Mexican

a collection of over 100 essential recipes

Bath · New York · Singapore · Hong Kong · Cologne · Delhi · Melbourne

This edition published by Parragon in 2010

Parragon
Chartist House
15-17 Trim Street
Bath BA1 1HA, UK
www.parragon.com

ISBN: 978-1-4454-1173-6

Printed in China

Designed by Terry Jeavons & Company

Notes for the Reader
This book uses imperial, metric, and US cup measurements. Follow the same units of measurement throughout; do not mix imperial and metric. All spoon measurements are level: teaspoons are assumed to be 5 ml, and tablespoons are assumed to be 15 ml. Unless otherwise stated, milk is assumed to be whole, eggs and individual vegetables such as potatoes are medium, and pepper is freshly ground black pepper.

The times given are an approximate guide only. Preparation times differ according to the techniques used by different people and the cooking times may also vary from those given as a result of the type of oven used. Optional ingredients, variations or serving suggestions have not been included in the calculations.

Recipes using raw or very lightly cooked eggs should be avoided by infants, the elderly, pregnant women, convalescents, and anyone with a chronic condition. Pregnant and breastfeeding women are advised to avoid eating peanuts and peanut products. Sufferers from nut allergies should be aware that some of the ready-prepared ingredients used in the recipes in this book may contain nuts. Always check the packaging before use.

Picture Acknowledgments
The publisher would like to thank the following for permission to reproduce copyright material on the following pages: Front cover: Green Chillies © John Shipes/Getty Images.

Mexican

introduction

The cuisine of Mexico is diverse and extraordinary and is fusion food at its most literal, having evolved from a complex layering of cultures. It began with the Indian civilizations and in later centuries was built on by the Spanish conquest as well as other European rulers and influences.

The soul of Mexican food lies in its ancient roots – Aztec, Toltec, Zapotec, Ohnec, and Mayan. From these roots come the deeply colored, rich sauces made of mild and hot chilies, seeds, herbs, and vegetables that are so characteristic of Mexican cuisine. Long-stewed meats are also a feature, while the broth that results

forms the basis for the soups that fuel everyday life and is used to add flavor and depth to stews, and to bean and rice dishes. Fish are flavored with spicy pastes or chilies, and served wrapped in tortillas or fragrant leaves.

To this ancient cuisine making use of the country's indigenous foods, the Spanish settlers added their own touch, not least of which was the pig – a useful source of meat now very popular in Mexican cooking, while the fat that comes from pork enabled frying to be used as an alternative cooking method. In addition, the Spanish brought wheat, used to make tortillas and crusty bread rolls, and domestic animals – cows, sheep, and goats – whose milk was used to make cheese.

The name Mexico conjures up a picture of sunshine, heat, color, and fiesta, and Mexican food reflects this – indeed, meals are a never-ending fiesta. The main meal is served Spanish style in the afternoon and follows a light breakfast of hot chocolate or coffee

with sweet rolls or cinnamon-sprinkled churros, or a substantial "brunch," often consisting of one of the country's well-known egg dishes. For in between there are markets and cafés selling tantalizing snacks. Eat Mexican-style, and soak up that party atmosphere!

something light

This chapter has a selection of some of Mexico's best soup and appetizer recipes, which you can use to form part of a Mexican-style feast for the family or serve on their own when you want a light lunch or supper dish that has just a little more character than the usual sandwich.

The soups are certainly packed with enough goodness to keep you full of energy, ranging from a light but very nutritious chilled avocado soup to Pozole, a protein-packed meal-in-a-bowl made from pork, chicken, and hominy (maize kernels) simmered in a rich stock. Mexican soups are served with plenty of garnishes, from a spoonful of soured cream, chunks of lime, and freshly chopped herbs to more complicated salsas, which complement the soup perfectly so are worth the extra effort.

Cheese and beans are a big feature of Mexican cuisine, and form the basis of Mexico's many exciting variations on the sandwich – tortillas, tostadas, quesadillas, tortas, and molletes. Fish and seafood are also very much in evidence, served in surprising ways – plump, juicy shrimp with smooth, sweet mango and a hint of mild chili, for example, an unusual but delightful combination. And you'll find some new and interesting ways to serve eggs, too.

mexican vegetable soup with tortilla chips

ingredients

SERVES 4–6

2 tbsp. vegetable or virgin
    olive oil
1 onion, finely chopped
4 garlic cloves, finely chopped
1/4–1/2 tsp. ground cumin
2–3 tsp. mild chili powder, such
    as ancho or New Mexico
1 carrot, sliced
1 waxy potato, diced
12 oz/350 g/1 1/2 cups diced
    fresh or canned tomatoes
1 zucchini, diced
1/4 small cabbage, shredded
1 3/4 pints/1 litre/4 cups
    vegetable or chicken stock
    or water
1 corn cob, the kernels cut off
    the cob
about 10 green or string beans,
    cut into bite-size lengths
salt and pepper

to serve

4–6 tbsp. chopped fresh cilantro
salsa of your choice or chopped
    fresh chili, to taste
tortilla chips

method

Heat the oil in a heavy-bottomed skillet or pan.
Add the onion and garlic and cook for a few minutes
until softened, then sprinkle in the cumin and chili
powder. Stir in the carrot, potato, tomatoes, zucchini,
and cabbage and cook for 2 minutes, stirring the
mixture occasionally.

Pour in the stock. Cover and cook over medium heat
for 20 minutes, or until the vegetables are tender.

Add extra water if necessary, then stir in the corn and
beans and cook for an additional 5–10 minutes, or until
the beans are tender. Season the soup to taste with salt
and pepper, bearing in mind that the tortilla chips may
be salty.

Ladle the soup into soup bowls and sprinkle each
portion with chopped cilantro. Top with a little salsa,
then add a handful of tortilla chips.

chilled avocado & cilantro soup

ingredients

SERVES 4

4 ripe avocados

1 shallot or 2 scallions, finely chopped

1½ pints/850ml/3½ cups cold chicken or strongly flavored vegetable stock

5 fl oz /150 ml/⅔ cup sour cream, plus extra to serve

2 tbsp. tomato paste

few drops of Tabasco sauce, or to taste

juice of 1 lime, or to taste

1 tbsp. tequila (optional)

1 tbsp. chopped fresh cilantro, plus extra to garnish

salt and pepper

method

Cut the avocados in half lengthwise and twist the two halves in opposite directions to separate. Stab the pit with the point of a sharp knife and lift out of the avocado.

Peel, then coarsely chop the avocado halves and place in a food processor or blender with the shallot, stock, sour cream, tomato paste, Tabasco, lime juice, tequila, chopped cilantro, and salt and pepper. Process until smooth, then taste and add more Tabasco, lime juice, and salt and pepper if necessary.

Transfer the mixture to a large bowl, cover, and let chill in the refrigerator for at least 2 hours, or until thoroughly chilled.

Divide the soup between four chilled serving bowls and serve, topped with a spoonful of sour cream and garnished with extra chopped cilantro.

easy gazpacho

ingredients

SERVES 4

1 small cucumber, peeled
   and chopped
2 red bell peppers, seeded
   and chopped
2 green bell peppers, seeded
   and chopped
2 garlic cloves, chopped
1 fresh basil sprig
$2^1/_2$ cups strained tomatoes
1 tbsp. extra-virgin olive oil
1 tbsp. red wine vinegar
1 tbsp. balsamic vinegar
10 fl oz/300 ml/$1^1/_4$ cups
   vegetable stock
2 tbsp. lemon juice
salt and pepper

to serve

2 tbsp. diced, peeled cucumber
2 tbsp. finely chopped red onion
2 tbsp. finely chopped red
   bell pepper
2 tbsp. finely chopped green
   bell pepper
ice cubes
4 fresh basil sprigs
fresh crusty bread

method

Put the cucumber, bell peppers, garlic, and basil in a food processor and process for $1^1/_2$ minutes. Add the strained tomatoes, olive oil, and both kinds of vinegar and process until smooth.

Pour in the vegetable stock and lemon juice and stir. Transfer the mixture to a large bowl. Season to taste with salt and pepper. Cover with plastic wrap and let chill in the refrigerator for at least 2 hours.

To serve, prepare the cucumber, onion, and bell peppers, then place in small serving dishes or arrange decoratively on a plate. Place ice cubes in four large soup bowls. Stir the soup and ladle it into the bowls. Garnish with the basil sprigs and serve with the prepared vegetables and chunks of fresh crusty bread.

beef and pea soup

ingredients

SERVES 4

2 tbsp. vegetable oil

1 large onion, finely chopped

2 garlic cloves, finely chopped

1 green bell pepper, seeded
and sliced

2 carrots, sliced

14 oz/400 g canned
black-eye peas

8 oz/225 g/1 cup fresh
ground beef

1 tsp. each of ground cumin,
chili powder, and paprika

1/4 cabbage, sliced

8 oz/225 g tomatoes, peeled
and chopped

1 pint/600 ml/2 1/2 cups beef
stock

salt and pepper

method

Heat the oil in a large pan over medium heat. Add the onion and garlic and cook, stirring frequently, for 5 minutes, or until softened. Add the bell pepper and carrots and cook for an additional 5 minutes.

Meanwhile, drain the peas, reserving the liquid from the can. Place two-thirds of the peas, reserving the remainder, in a food processor or blender with the pea liquid and process until smooth.

Add the ground beef to the pan and cook, stirring constantly to break up any lumps, until well browned. Add the spices and cook, stirring, for 2 minutes. Add the cabbage, tomatoes, stock, and puréed peas and season to taste with salt and pepper. Bring to a boil, then reduce the heat, cover, and let simmer for 15 minutes, or until the vegetables are tender.

Stir in the reserved peas, cover, and let simmer for an additional 5 minutes. Ladle the soup into warmed soup bowls and serve.

pozole

ingredients

SERVES 4

1 lb/450 g pork for stewing,
    such as lean belly

$^1/_2$ small chicken

about $3^1/_2$ pints/2 litres/
    8 cups water

1 chicken bouillon cube

1 whole garlic bulb, divided
    into cloves but not peeled

1 onion, chopped

2 bay leaves

1 lb/450 g canned or cooked
    hominy or chickpeas

$^1/_4$–$^1/_2$ tsp. ground cumin

salt and pepper

to serve

$^1/_2$ small cabbage, thinly
    shredded

fried pork skin

dried oregano leaves

dried chili flakes

lime wedges

tortilla chips (optional)

method

Place the pork and chicken in a large pan. Add enough water to fill the pan. (Do not worry about having too much stock – it can be used in other dishes, and freezes well.) Bring to a boil, then skim off the scum that rises to the surface. Reduce the heat and add the bouillon cube, garlic, onion, and bay leaves. Simmer, covered, over medium–low heat for $1^1/_2$–2 hours, or until the pork and chicken are both tender and cooked through.

Using a slotted spoon, remove the pork and chicken from the soup and let cool. When cool enough to handle, remove the chicken flesh from the bones and cut into small pieces. Cut the pork into bite-size pieces. Set aside.

Skim the fat off the soup and discard the bay leaves. Add the hominy or chickpeas, cumin, and salt and pepper to taste. Bring to a boil.

To serve, place a little pork and chicken in soup bowls. Top with cabbage, fried pork skin, oregano, and chili flakes, then spoon in the hot soup. Serve with lime wedges and tortilla chips, if wished.

chicken, avocado & chipotle soup

ingredients

SERVES 4

2³/₄ pints/1.5 litres/6¹/₄cups
    chicken stock
2–3 garlic cloves, finely
    chopped
1–2 dried chipotle chiles, cut
    into very thin strips
1 avocado
lime or lemon juice, for tossing
3–5 scallions, thinly sliced
12–14 oz/350–400 g cooked
    chicken breast meat, torn or
    cut into shreds or thin strips
2 tbsp. chopped fresh cilantro

to serve
1 lime, cut into wedges
handful of tortilla chips
    (optional)

method

Place the stock in a large, heavy-bottomed pan with the garlic and chiles and bring to a boil.

Meanwhile, cut the avocado in half around the pit. Twist apart, then remove the pit with a knife. Carefully peel off the skin, dice the flesh, and toss in lime juice to prevent discoloration.

Arrange the scallions, chicken, avocado, and cilantro in the bottom of four soup bowls or in a large serving bowl.

Ladle hot stock over and serve with lime wedges and a handful of tortilla chips, if wished.

mexican fish & roasted tomato soup

ingredients

SERVES 4

5 ripe tomatoes

5 garlic cloves, unpeeled

1 lb 2 oz/500 g red snapper, cut into chunks

1³/₄ pints/1 litre/4 cups fish stock or water mixed with 1–2 fish bouillon cubes

2–3 tbsp. olive oil

1 onion, chopped

2 fresh green chiles, such as serrano, seeded and thinly sliced

lime wedges, to serve

method

Heat an unoiled heavy-bottomed skillet. Add the tomatoes and garlic and char over high heat or under a preheated hot broiler. The skins of the vegetables should blacken and the flesh inside should be tender. Alternatively, place the tomatoes and garlic in a roasting pan and bake in a preheated oven at 375°F/190°C for 40 minutes.

Let the tomatoes and garlic cool, then remove the skins and coarsely chop, combining them with any juices from the skillet or roasting pan. Set aside.

Poach the fish in the stock in a deep skillet or pan over medium heat until it is just opaque and slightly firm. Remove from the heat and set aside.

Heat the oil in a separate deep skillet or pan. Add the onion and cook for 5 minutes, or until softened. Strain in the cooking liquid from the fish, then stir in the tomatoes and garlic.

Bring to a boil, then reduce the heat and simmer for 5 minutes to combine the flavors. Add the chiles.

Divide chunks of the poached fish between soup bowls, ladle over the hot soup, and serve with lime wedges for squeezing over the top.

spicy fragrant black bean chili

ingredients

SERVES 4

14 oz/400 g/2¼ cups dried
   black beans
2 tbsp. olive oil
1 onion, chopped
5 garlic cloves, coarsely
   chopped
2 bacon strips, diced (optional)
¹/₂–1 tsp. ground cumin
¹/₂–1 tsp. mild red chili powder
1 red bell pepper, diced
1 carrot, diced
14 oz/400 g fresh tomatoes,
   diced, or canned, chopped
1 bunch fresh cilantro,
   coarsely chopped
salt and pepper

method

Soak the beans overnight, then drain. Place in a pan, cover with water, and bring to a boil. Boil for 10 minutes, then reduce the heat and simmer for 1¹/₂ hours, or until tender. Drain well, reserving 1 cup of the cooking liquid.

Heat the oil in a skillet. Add the onion and garlic and cook for 2 minutes, stirring. Add the bacon, if using, and cook, stirring occasionally, until the bacon is cooked and the onion is softened.

Stir in the cumin and chili powder and continue to cook for a moment or two. Add the red bell pepper, carrot, and tomatoes. Cook over medium heat for 5 minutes.

Add half the cilantro and the beans and their reserved liquid. Season to taste with salt and pepper. Simmer for 30–45 minutes, or until very flavorful and thickened.

Stir in the remaining cilantro, adjust the seasoning, and serve at once.

shrimp & mango cocktail

ingredients

SERVES 4

6 cherry tomatoes

1 large ripe mango

1 fresh mild green chili,
    seeded and finely chopped

juice of 1 lime

1 tbsp. chopped fresh cilantro

salt and pepper

14 oz/400 g shelled jumbo
    shrimp, cooked

fresh cilantro, chopped,
    to garnish

method

Place the tomatoes in a heatproof bowl and pour over enough boiling water to cover. Let stand for 1–2 minutes, then remove the tomatoes with a slotted spoon, peel off the skins, and refresh in cold water. Dice the flesh and place in a large, nonmetallic bowl.

Slice the mango lengthwise on either side of the flat central seed. Peel the two mango pieces and cut the flesh into chunks. Slice and peel any remaining flesh around the seed, then cut into chunks. Add to the tomatoes with any juice.

Add the chili, lime juice, chopped cilantro, and salt and pepper to taste. Cover and let chill in the refrigerator for 2 hours to allow the flavors to develop.

Remove the dish from the refrigerator. Fold the shrimp gently into the mango mixture and divide between 4 serving dishes. Garnish with chopped cilantro and serve at once.

seafood cocktail à la Veracruz

ingredients

SERVES 6

1³/₄ pints/1 litre/4 cups fish
    stock or water mixed with
    1 fish bouillon cube
2 bay leaves
1 onion, chopped
3–5 garlic cloves, cut into
    big chunks
1 lb 8 oz/675 g mixed raw
    seafood, such as shrimp
    in their shells, scallops,
    squid rings, pieces of
    squid tentacles, etc.
6 fl oz/175 ml/³/₄ cup tomato
    ketchup
4 tbsp. Mexican hot sauce
generous pinch of ground
    cumin
6–8 tbsp. chopped fresh
    cilantro
4 tbsp. lime juice, plus extra
    for tossing
salt
1 avocado, to garnish

method

Place the stock in a large, heavy-bottomed pan and add the bay leaves, half the onion, and all the garlic. Bring to a boil, then reduce the heat and simmer for 10 minutes, or until the onion and garlic are soft and the stock tastes flavorful.

Add the seafood in the order of the amount of cooking time required. Most small pieces of shellfish take a very short time to cook, and can be added together. Cook for 1 minute, then remove the pan from the heat. Allow the seafood to finish cooking by standing in the cooling stock.

When the stock has cooled, remove the seafood from the stock with a slotted spoon. Shell the shrimp and any other shellfish. Set the stock aside until required.

Combine the ketchup, hot sauce, and cumin in a bowl. Reserve a quarter of the sauce mixture for serving. Add the seafood to the bowl with the remaining onion, cilantro, lime juice, and about 1 cup of the reserved fish stock. Stir carefully to mix and season to taste with salt.

Peel and pit the avocado, then dice the flesh. Toss gently in lime juice to prevent discoloration. Serve the cocktail in individual bowls, garnished with the avocado, and topped with a spoonful of the reserved sauce.

cheese & bean quesadillas

ingredients

SERVES 4–6

8 flour tortillas (see page 206)

vegetable oil, for oiling

1/2 quantity refried beans (see page 202), warmed with a little water

7 oz/200 g Cheddar cheese, grated

1 onion, chopped

1/2 bunch fresh cilantro leaves, chopped, plus extra leaves to garnish (optional)

1 quantity Salsa Cruda (see page 168)

method

First make the tortillas pliable, by warming them gently in a lightly oiled nonstick skillet.

Remove the tortillas from the skillet and quickly spread with a layer of warmed beans. Top each tortilla with grated cheese, onion, cilantro, and a spoonful of salsa. Roll up tightly.

Just before serving, heat the nonstick skillet over medium heat, sprinkling lightly with a drop or two of water. Add the tortilla rolls, cover the skillet, and heat through until the cheese melts. Allow to lightly brown, if wished.

Remove from the skillet and slice each roll, on the diagonal, into about 4 bite-size pieces. Serve the dish at once, garnished with cilantro, if wished.

nachos

ingredients

SERVES 6

6 oz/175 g tortilla chips

1 quantity warmed refried
   beans (see page 202)
   or 14 oz/400 g canned
   refried beans, warmed

2 tbsp. finely chopped bottled
   jalapeño chilies

7 oz/200 g canned or bottled
   pimientos or roasted bell
   peppers, drained and
   finely sliced

salt and pepper

4 oz/115 g Gruyère cheese,
   grated

4 oz/115 g Cheddar cheese,
   grated

method

Preheat the oven to 400°F/200°C.

Spread the tortilla chips out over the bottom of a large, shallow, ovenproof dish or roasting pan. Cover with the warmed refried beans. Sprinkle over the chilies and pimientos and season to taste with salt and pepper.

Mix the cheeses together in a bowl and sprinkle on top.

Bake in the preheated oven for 5–8 minutes, or until the cheese is bubbling and melted. Serve at once.

roasted cheese with salsa

ingredients

SERVES 4

8 oz/225 g mozzarella, fresh romano, or Mexican queso oaxaca cheese

6 fl oz/175 ml/3/4 cup Salsa Cruda (see page 168) or other good salsa

1/2–1 onion, finely chopped

8 soft corn tortillas, to serve

method

Preheat the oven to 400°F/200°C or preheat the broiler to medium. To warm the tortillas ready for serving, heat an unoiled nonstick skillet, add a tortilla, and heat through, sprinkling with a few drops of water as it heats. Wrap in foil or a clean dish towel to keep warm. Repeat with the other tortillas.

Cut the cheese into chunks or slabs and arrange them in a shallow ovenproof dish or in individual dishes.

Spoon the salsa over the cheese to cover and place in the preheated oven or under the hot broiler. Cook until the cheese melts and is bubbling, lightly browning in places.

Sprinkle with chopped onion to taste and serve with the warmed tortillas for dipping. Serve immediately as the melted cheese turns stringy when cold and becomes difficult to eat.

tamales

ingredients

SERVES 4–6

8–10 corn husks or several
  banana leaves, cut into
  12-inch/30-cm squares
6 tbsp. shortening
1/2 tsp. salt
pinch of sugar
pinch of ground cumin
8 oz/225 g masa harina
1/2 tsp. baking powder
about 8 fl oz/225 ml/1 cup
  beef, chicken, or
  vegetable stock

filling

4 oz/115 g/1 cup cooked corn
  kernels, mixed with grated
  cheese and chopped fresh
  green chili, or pork simmered
  in a mild chili sauce

to serve

shredded lettuce
tomato wedges
salsa of your choice

method

If using corn husks, soak in enough hot water to cover
for at least 3 hours or overnight. If using banana leaves,
warm them by placing over an open flame for just a few
seconds, to make them pliable.

To make the tamale dough, beat the shortening until fluffy in
a bowl, then beat in the salt, sugar, cumin, masa harina, and
baking powder until the mixture resembles very fine crumbs.

Add the stock very gradually, in several batches,
beating until the mixture becomes fluffy and resembles
whipped cream.

Spread 1–2 tablespoons of the tamale mixture on either
a soaked and drained corn husk or a piece of pliable
heated banana leaf.

Spoon in the filling. Fold the sides of the husks or leaves
over the filling to enclose. Wrap each pocket in a square
of foil and arrange in a steamer.

Pour enough hot water into the bottom of the steamer,
cover, and boil. Steam for 40–60 minutes, topping up
the water in the bottom of the steamer when needed.
Remove the tamales and serve with shredded lettuce,
tomato wedges, and salsa.

molletes

ingredients

SERVES 4

4 bread rolls

1 tbsp. vegetable oil, plus
extra for brushing

14 oz/400 g refried beans
(see page 202) or canned

1 onion, chopped

3 garlic cloves, chopped

3 bacon strips, cut into small
pieces, or about 3 oz/85 g
chorizo sausage, diced

8 oz/225 g diced fresh or
canned tomatoes

1/4–1/2 tsp. ground cumin

9 oz/250 g/21/4 cups grated
cheese

cabbage salad

1/2 cabbage, thinly sliced

2 tbsp. sliced pickled
jalapeño chilies

1 tbsp. extra-virgin olive oil

3 tbsp. cider vinegar

1/4 tsp. dried oregano

salt and pepper

method

Preheat the oven to 400°F/200°C. Cut the rolls in half and remove a little of the crumb to make space for the filling.

To make the salad, combine the cabbage with the chilies, olive oil, and vinegar in a bowl. Add the oregano and salt and pepper to taste. Set aside.

Brush the rolls all over with vegetable oil. Arrange on a cookie sheet and bake in the preheated oven for 10–15 minutes, or until the rolls are crisp and light golden.

Meanwhile, place the beans in a pan and heat through gently with enough water to thin them to a smooth paste.

Heat the 1 tablespoon of vegetable oil in a skillet. Add the onion, garlic, and bacon or chorizo and cook until the bacon or chorizo is browned and the onion is softened. Add the tomatoes and simmer, stirring, until they break down to form a thick sauce.

Add the warmed beans to the skillet and stir to combine with the mixture. Stir in the cumin to taste. Set aside.

Remove the rolls from the oven; keep the oven on. Fill the rolls with the warm bean mixture, then top with the cheese and close up tightly. Return to the cookie sheet and heat through in the oven until the cheese melts.

Open the rolls up and spoon in a little of the salad. Serve immediately.

tortas

ingredients

SERVES 4

4 crusty rolls, such as French
    rolls or bocadillos
melted butter or olive oil, for
    brushing
1 cup/8 oz/225 g refried
    beans or canned
12 oz/350 g/1½ cups
    shredded cooked chicken,
    browned chorizo sausage
    pieces, sliced ham, and
    cheese or any leftover
    cooked meat you have
    to hand
1 ripe tomato, sliced or diced
1 small onion, finely chopped
2 tbsp. chopped fresh cilantro
1 avocado, pitted, peeled,
    sliced, and tossed with
    lime juice
4–6 tbsp. sour cream or
    strained plain yogurt
salsa of your choice
handful of shredded lettuce

method

Cut the rolls in half and, using your fingers, remove a
little of the crumb to make space for the filling.

Brush the outside and inside of the rolls with butter and
toast, on both sides, in a hot grill pan or skillet for a few
minutes until crisp. Alternatively, preheat the oven to
400°F/200°C and bake until lightly toasted.

Meanwhile, place the beans in a pan with a tiny amount
of water and heat through gently.

When the rolls are heated, spread one half of each roll
generously with the beans, then top with a layer of cooked
meat. Top with tomato, onion, cilantro, and avocado.

Generously spread sour cream on to the other side of
each roll. Drizzle the salsa over the filling, add a little
shredded lettuce, then sandwich the two sides of each
roll together; press tightly. Serve immediately.

chicken tortilla flutes with guacamole

ingredients

SERVES 4

8 soft corn tortillas

12 oz/350 g cooked chicken, diced

1 tsp. mild chili powder

1 onion, chopped

2 tbsp. finely chopped fresh cilantro

salt

1–2 tbsp. sour cream

vegetable oil, for frying

to serve

guacamole (see page 152)

salsa of your choice

method

Heat the tortillas in an unoiled nonstick skillet in a stack, moving the tortillas from the top to the bottom so that they warm evenly. Wrap in foil or a clean dish towel to keep them warm.

Place the chicken in a large bowl with the chili powder, half the chopped onion and cilantro, and salt to taste. Add enough sour cream to bind the mixture together.

Arrange 2 corn tortillas on the counter so that they are overlapping, then spoon some of the filling down the center. Roll up very tightly and secure in place with a toothpick or two. Repeat with the remaining tortillas and filling.

Heat enough oil for frying in a deep skillet until hot and fry the rolls until golden and crisp. Carefully remove the rolls from the oil and drain on paper towels.

Serve with the guacamole, salsa, and the remaining onion and cilantro.

stuffed tortillas

ingredients

SERVES 2

4 sausages

salsa

2 red bell peppers, seeded
and cut into fourths

11 1/2 oz/325 g canned red
kidney beans, drained,
rinsed, and drained again

4 large tomatoes, chopped

1 large onion, chopped

1 garlic clove, chopped

1 tbsp. lime juice

1 tbsp. chopped fresh basil

salt and pepper

4 large wheat or corn tortillas,
or 8 small ones

salad, to garnish

to serve

shredded lettuce

slices of fresh tomato

sour cream

method

Cook the red bell peppers, skin-side up, under a preheated broiler for about 5 minutes, or until the skins are blackened and charred. Transfer them to a plastic bag, seal the bag, and set to one side.

Broil the sausages for 10–12 minutes, or until cooked right through, turning occasionally. While the sausages are cooking, put the kidney beans, tomatoes, onion, garlic, lime juice, and basil into a large bowl. Season with salt and pepper and mix until well combined.

Take the red bell pepper fourths from the plastic bag and remove the blackened skins. Chop the flesh into small pieces and add it to the kidney bean mixture. Meanwhile, warm the tortillas in an unoiled nonstick skillet in a stack, moving the tortillas from the top to the bottom so that they warm evenly. Wrap in foil or a clean dish towel to keep them warm.

Cut the sausages into slices. Fill the tortillas with sausage slices, kidney bean salsa, shredded lettuce, tomato slices, and sour cream. Serve at once with a salad garnish.

vegetable tostadas

ingredients

SERVES 4

4 soft corn tortillas

2–3 tbsp. or vegetable oil, plus extra for frying

2 potatoes, diced

1 carrot, diced

3 garlic cloves, finely chopped

1 red bell pepper, seeded and diced

1 tsp. mild chili powder

1 tsp. paprika

$1/2$ tsp. ground cumin

3–4 ripe tomatoes, diced

4 oz/115 g green beans, blanched and cut into bite-size lengths

several large pinches of dried oregano

14 oz/400 g cooked black beans, drained

8 oz/225 g/2 cups crumbled feta cheese

3–4 romaine lettuce leaves, shredded

3–4 scallions, thinly sliced

method

To make the tostadas, fry the tortillas in a small amount of oil in a nonstick skillet until crisp. Set aside.

Heat the remaining oil in the skillet. Add the potatoes and carrot and cook for 10 minutes, or until softened. Add the garlic, red bell pepper, chili powder, paprika, and cumin. Cook for 2–3 minutes, or until the bell peppers have softened.

Add the tomatoes, green beans, and oregano. Cook for 8–10 minutes, or until the vegetables are tender and form a sauce-like mixture. The mixture should not be too dry; add a little water if necessary to keep it moist.

Preheat the broiler to medium. Heat the black beans in a pan with a tiny amount of water and keep warm. Reheat the tostadas under the hot broiler.

Layer the beans over the hot tostadas, then sprinkle with the cheese and top with a few spoonfuls of the hot vegetables in sauce. Sprinkle each tostada with the lettuce and scallions and serve at once.

spinach & mushroom chimichangas

ingredients

SERVES 4

2 tbsp. olive oil

1 large onion, finely chopped

8 oz/225 g small mushrooms, finely sliced

2 fresh mild green chilies, seeded and finely chopped

2 garlic cloves, finely chopped

9 oz/250 g/8 cups spinach leaves, torn into pieces if large

6 oz/175 g Cheddar cheese, grated

8 flour tortillas (see page 206), warmed

vegetable oil, for deep-frying

method

Heat the oil in a large, heavy-bottom skillet. Add the onion and cook over medium heat for 5 minutes, or until softened.

Add the mushrooms, chilies, and garlic and cook for 5 minutes, or until the mushrooms are lightly browned. Add the spinach and cook, stirring, for 1–2 minutes, or until just wilted. Add the cheese and stir until just melted.

Spoon an equal quantity of the mixture into the center of each tortilla. Fold in two opposite sides of each tortilla to cover the filling, then roll up to enclose it completely.

Heat the oil for deep-frying in a deep-fryer or large, deep pan to 350–375°F/180–190°C, or until a cube of bread browns in 30 seconds. Deep-fry the chimichangas two at a time, turning once, for 5–6 minutes, or until crisp and golden. Drain on paper towels before serving.

cheese enchiladas with mole flavors

ingredients

SERVES 4

8 soft corn tortillas

vegetable oil, for oiling

16 fl oz/450 ml/2 cups mole
poblano (see page 158)
or bottled mole paste

about 8 oz/225 g/2 cups
grated cheese, such as
Cheddar, mozzarella,
Asiago, or Mexican queso
oaxaco—one type or a
combination

8 fl oz/225 ml/1 cup chicken
or vegetable stock

5 scallions, thinly sliced

2–3 tbsp. chopped fresh
cilantro

handful of romaine lettuce
leaves, shredded

1 avocado, pitted, peeled,
diced, and tossed in
lime juice

4 tbsp. sour cream

salsa of your choice

method

Preheat the oven to 375°F/190°C. Heat the tortillas in a lightly oiled nonstick skillet; wrap in foil or a clean dish towel as you work to keep them warm.

Dip the tortillas into the mole sauce and pile up on a plate. Fill the inside of the top sauced tortilla with a few spoonfuls of grated cheese. Roll up and arrange in a shallow ovenproof dish. Repeat with the remaining tortillas, reserving a handful of the cheese to sprinkle over the top.

Pour the rest of the mole sauce over the rolled tortillas, then pour the stock over the top. Sprinkle with the reserved cheese and cover with foil.

Bake in the preheated oven for 20 minutes, or until the tortillas are piping hot and the cheese filling melts.

Arrange the scallions, cilantro, lettuce, avocado, and sour cream on top. Add salsa to taste. Serve at once.

jalisco-style eggs

ingredients

SERVES 4

4 soft corn tortillas

1 avocado

lime or lemon juice, for tossing

6 oz/175 g fresh chorizo
    sausage, sliced or diced

2 tbsp. butter or water,
    for cooking

4 eggs

4 tbsp. crumbled feta cheese

salsa of your choice

1 tbsp. chopped fresh cilantro

1 tbsp. finely chopped scallions

method

Heat the tortillas in an unoiled nonstick skillet, sprinkling them with a few drops of water as they heat; wrap the tortillas in foil or a clean dish towel as you work to keep them warm. Alternatively, heat through in a stack in the skillet, moving the tortillas from the top to the bottom so that they warm evenly. Wrap to keep them warm.

Cut the avocado in half around the pit. Twist apart, then remove the pit with a knife. Carefully peel off the skin, dice the flesh, and toss in lime juice to prevent discoloration.

Heat a separate skillet, add the chorizo, and cook until browned, then arrange on each warmed tortilla. Keep warm.

Meanwhile, heat the butter or water in the nonstick skillet, break in an egg, and cook until the white is set but the yolk is still soft. Remove from the skillet and place on top of one tortilla. Keep warm.

Cook the remaining eggs in the same way, adding to the tortillas.

Arrange the avocado, cheese, and a spoonful of salsa on each tortilla. Add the cilantro and scallions and serve.

huevos rancheros

ingredients

SERVES 4

2 tbsp. butter, bacon fat, or lard

2 onions, finely chopped

2 garlic cloves, finely chopped

2 red or yellow bell peppers,
seeded and diced

2 fresh mild green chilies,
seeded and finely chopped

4 large ripe tomatoes, peeled
and chopped

2 tbsp. lemon or lime juice

2 tsp. dried oregano

salt and pepper

4 large eggs

3 oz/75 g Cheddar cheese,
grated

method

Preheat the oven to 350°F/180°C. Heat the butter in a heavy-bottom skillet over medium heat. Add the onions and garlic and cook, stirring frequently, for 5 minutes, or until softened. Add the bell peppers and chilies and cook for 5 minutes, until softened.

Add the tomatoes, lemon juice, and oregano and season to taste with salt and pepper. Bring to a boil, then reduce the heat, cover, and let simmer for 10 minutes, or until thickened, adding a little more lemon juice if the mixture becomes too dry.

Transfer the mixture to a large, ovenproof dish. Make four hollows in the mixture and break an egg into each. Bake in the preheated oven for 12–15 minutes, or until the eggs are set.

Sprinkle with grated cheese and return to the oven for 3–4 minutes, or until the cheese has melted. Serve at once.

eggs oaxaca-style

ingredients

SERVES 4

2 lb 4 oz/1 kg ripe tomatoes
about 12 pearl onions, halved
8 garlic cloves, whole and
    unpeeled
2 fresh mild green chilies
pinch of ground cumin
pinch of dried oregano
salt and pepper
pinch of sugar (optional)
2–3 tsp. vegetable oil
8 eggs, lightly beaten
1–2 tbsp. tomato paste
1–2 tbsp. chopped fresh
    cilantro, to garnish

method

Heat an unoiled heavy-based skillet. Add the tomatoes and char lightly, turning them once or twice. Remove from the skillet and let cool.

Meanwhile, lightly char the onions, garlic, and chilies in the skillet. Remove from the skillet and let cool slightly.

Cut the cooled tomatoes into pieces and place in a food processor or blender with their charred skins. Remove the stalks and seeds from the chilies, then peel and chop. Remove the skins from the garlic, then chop. Coarsely chop the onions. Add the chopped chilies, garlic, and onions to the tomatoes.

Process to make a coarse purée, then add the cumin and oregano. Season to taste with salt and pepper and add sugar, if necessary.

Heat the oil in a nonstick skillet. Add a ladleful of egg and cook to make a thin omelet. Continue to make omelets, stacking them on a plate as they are cooked. Slice into noodle-like ribbons.

Bring the sauce to a boil in a pan and adjust the seasoning, adding tomato paste to taste. Add the omelet strips, warm through, then serve at once, garnished with a sprinkling of cilantro.

made with meat

National cuisine is all about making creative use of the local produce, and Mexico is no exception. Beef, pork, and chicken are all used, avocados make frequent appearances, and then there is tequila, the now world-famous local liquor that is excellent as a meat tenderizer. And chocolate … not in every recipe, of course, but it seems that meat and chocolate marry remarkably well, so do be adventurous and try adding a little to a steak chili, or make the Chicken Mole Poblano illustrated here.

In Mexico the main meal is traditionally served at midday and is a gloriously relaxed affair, usually with a meat or fish dish for the central course. Meat dishes are often cooked very slowly, either as a stew or in the oven, as a casserole. And virtually every dish will contain the ingredient that, along with tortillas and beans, defines Mexican food – chilies. They are eaten raw and cooked, sliced and stewed, stuffed and puréed, soaked and fried, and appear at every meal to add flavor, texture, color and aroma. Some recipes call for nothing more than a hint of mild chili powder, while two of the fresh version of the milder chilies – anaheim and poblano – are perfect for stuffing. Other recipes use chilies that start hot and get hotter, so be warned – they are fire for your tastebuds!

steak, avocado & bean salad

ingredients

SERVES 4–6

12 oz/350 g tender steak,
    such as sirloin
4 garlic cloves, chopped
juice of 1 lime
4 tbsp. extra-virgin olive oil
salt and pepper
1 tbsp. white or red wine vinegar
1/4 tsp. mild chili powder
1/4 tsp. ground cumin
1/2 tsp. paprika
5 scallions, thinly sliced
about 7 oz/200 g crisp lettuce
    leaves, such as romaine
8 oz/225 g canned corn
    kernels, drained
14 oz/400 g canned pinto,
    black, or red kidney
    beans, drained
1 avocado, pitted, peeled,
    sliced, and tossed with a
    little lime juice
2 ripe tomatoes, diced
1/4 fresh green or red chili,
    chopped
3 tbsp. chopped fresh cilantro
generous handful of crisp tortilla
    chips, broken into pieces

method

Place the steak in a nonmetallic dish with the garlic and half the lime juice and oil. Season to taste with salt and pepper, cover, and let marinate for 30 minutes.

To make the dressing, combine the remaining lime juice and oil with the vinegar, chili powder, cumin, and paprika in a small nonmetallic bowl, then set aside.

Pan-fry the steak, or cook under a preheated very hot broiler, until browned on the outside and cooked to your liking in the middle. Transfer to a board, cut into strips, and reserve; keep warm or let cool.

Toss the scallions with the lettuce and arrange on a serving platter. Pour half the dressing over the leaves, then arrange the corn, beans, avocado, and tomatoes over the top. Sprinkle with the chili and cilantro.

Arrange the steak and the tortilla chips on top, pour over the rest of the dressing, and serve at once.

tequila-marinated beef steaks

ingredients

SERVES 4

2 tbsp. olive oil

3 tbsp. tequila

3 tbsp. freshly squeezed
orange juice

1 tbsp. freshly squeezed
lime juice

3 garlic cloves, crushed

2 tsp. chili powder

2 tsp. ground cumin

1 tsp. dried oregano

salt and pepper

4 sirloin steaks

method

Place the oil, tequila, orange and lime juices, garlic, chili powder, cumin, oregano, and salt and pepper to taste in a large, shallow, nonmetallic dish and mix together. Add the steaks and turn to coat in the marinade. Cover and let chill in the refrigerator for at least 2 hours or overnight, turning occasionally.

Preheat the barbecue and oil the grill rack. Let the steaks return to room temperature, then remove from the marinade. Cook over hot coals for 3–4 minutes on each side for medium, or longer according to taste, basting frequently with the marinade. Serve at once.

michoacan beef

ingredients

SERVES 4

about 3 tbsp. all-purpose flour

salt and pepper

2 lb 4 oz/1 kg stewing beef, cut
　　into large bite-size pieces

2 tbsp. vegetable oil

2 onions, chopped

5 garlic cloves, chopped

14 oz/400 g tomatoes, diced

1^1/$_2$ dried chipotle chilies,
　　reconstituted, seeded, and
　　cut into thin strips, or a
　　few shakes of bottled
　　chipotle salsa

2^3/$_4$ pints/1.5 litres/6^1/$_4$ cups
　　beef stock

12 oz/350 g green beans

pinch of sugar

to serve

simmered beans

freshly cooked rice

method

Place the flour in a large bowl and season to taste with salt and pepper. Add the beef and toss to coat well. Remove the beef from the bowl, shaking off the excess flour.

Heat the oil in a skillet. Add the beef and brown briefly over high heat. Reduce the heat to medium, add the onions and garlic, and cook for 2 minutes.

Add the tomatoes, chilies, and stock, then cover and simmer over low heat for 1^1/$_2$ hours, or until the meat is very tender, adding the green beans and sugar 15 minutes before the end of the cooking time. Skim off any fat that rises to the surface every now and again.

Transfer to individual bowls and serve with simmered beans and rice.

lone star chili

ingredients

SERVES 4

1 tbsp. cumin seeds

1 lb 7 oz/650 g rump steak, cut into 1-inch/2.5-cm cubes

all-purpose flour, well seasoned with salt and pepper, for coating

3 tbsp. beef drippings, bacon fat, or vegetable oil

2 onions, finely chopped

4 garlic cloves, finely chopped

1 tbsp. dried oregano

2 tsp. paprika

4 dried red chilies, such as ancho or pasilla, crushed, or to taste

1 large bottle of South American lager

4 squares semisweet chocolate

method

Dry-fry the cumin seeds in a heavy-bottom skillet over medium heat, shaking the skillet, for 3–4 minutes, or until lightly toasted. Let cool, then grind in a mortar with a pestle. Alternatively, use a coffee grinder reserved for the purpose.

Toss the beef in the seasoned flour to coat. Melt the fat in a large, heavy-bottom pan. Add the beef, in batches, and cook until browned on all sides. Remove the beef with a slotted spoon and set aside.

Add the onions and garlic to the pan and cook gently for 5 minutes, or until softened. Add the cumin, oregano, paprika, and chilies and cook, stirring, for 2 minutes. Return the beef to the pan, pour over the lager, then add the chocolate. Bring to a boil, stirring, then reduce the heat, cover, and let simmer for 2–3 hours, or until the beef is very tender, adding more lager if necessary.

chilies stuffed with beef

ingredients

SERVES 4

4 large fresh poblano chilies
all-purpose flour, for dusting
vegetable oil, for frying

spicy beef filling

1 lb 2 oz/500 g ground beef
1 onion, finely chopped
3 garlic cloves, finely chopped
4 tbsp. dry or sweet sherry
pinch of ground cinnamon
pinch of ground cloves
pinch of ground cumin
salt and pepper
14 oz/400 g canned chopped
　　tomatoes
1–3 tsp. sugar
1 tbsp. vinegar
3 tbsp. chopped fresh cilantro
2–3 tbsp. coarsely chopped
　　toasted almonds
Quick Tomato Sauce (see
　　page 162), to serve

batter

3 eggs, separated
6–8 tbsp. all-purpose flour
pinch of salt
4 fl oz/120 ml/ 1/2 cup water

method

Preheat the broiler to medium. Roast the chilies under the hot broiler until the skin is charred. Place in a plastic bag, twist to seal well, and let stand for 20 minutes. Make a slit in the side of each chili and remove the seeds, leaving the stalks intact. Set aside.

To make the filling, brown the meat and onion together in a heavy-bottomed skillet over medium heat. Pour off any extra fat, then add the garlic and sherry and boil down until the liquid has nearly evaporated.

Add the cinnamon, cloves, cumin, and salt and pepper to taste. Stir in the tomatoes, sugar, and vinegar and cook over medium heat until the tomatoes have reduced to a thick, strongly flavored sauce.

Stir in the cilantro and almonds and heat through. Stuff as much of the filling into the chilies as will fit, then dust each with flour. Set aside.

To make the batter, in a large bowl, lightly beat the egg yolks with the flour, salt, and enough of the water to make a thick mixture. In a separate bowl, whisk the egg whites until they form stiff peaks. Fold the egg whites into the batter, then gently dip each stuffed chili into the batter.

Heat the oil in a deep skillet until very hot and just smoking. Add the chilies and fry until they are golden brown. Serve hot, topped with the Quick Tomato Sauce.

classic beef fajitas

ingredients

SERVES 4–6

1 lb 9 oz/700 g sirloin steak
 or other tender beef steak,
 cut into strips
3 garlic cloves, chopped
juice of 1 lime
large pinch of mild chili powder
large pinch of paprika
large pinch of ground cumin
1–2 tbsp. extra-virgin olive oil
salt and pepper
12 flour tortillas (see page
 206)
vegetable oil, for oiling
 and frying
1–2 avocados, pitted, peeled,
 diced, and tossed with
 lime juice
4 fl oz/120 ml/$\frac{1}{2}$ cup sour
 cream

salsa

8 ripe tomatoes, diced
3 scallions, sliced
1–2 fresh green chilies,
 seeded and chopped
3–4 tbsp. chopped fresh
 cilantro
5–8 radishes, diced
ground cumin, to taste
salt and pepper

method

Combine the strips of steak with the garlic, half the lime
juice (toss the avocados in the remaining juice when
ready to serve, see ingredients), the chili powder,
paprika, cumin, and oil. Add salt and pepper to taste
and mix well. Cover and let marinate for at least 30
minutes at room temperature, or overnight in the
refrigerator.

To make the pico de gallo salsa, place the tomatoes in a
bowl with the scallions, chilies, cilantro, and radishes.
Season to taste with cumin, salt, and pepper. Set aside.

Heat the tortillas in a lightly oiled nonstick skillet; wrap in
foil or a clean dish towel as you work to keep them warm.

Heat a little oil in a large skillet or preheated wok. Add
the beef and stir-fry over high heat until browned and
just cooked through.

Serve the sizzling hot meat with the warmed tortillas, salsa,
avocado, and sour cream for each person to make his or
her own rolled-up fajitas.

beef enchiladas

ingredients

SERVES 4

2 tbsp. olive oil, plus extra
  for oiling
2 large onions, thinly sliced
1 lb 4 oz/550 g lean beef,
  cut into bite-size pieces
1 tbsp. ground cumin
1–2 tsp. cayenne pepper,
  or to taste
1 tsp. paprika
salt and pepper
8 soft corn tortillas
1 quantity taco sauce,
  warmed, and thinned with
  a little water if necessary
8 oz/225 g Cheddar cheese,
  grated

method

Preheat the oven to 350°F/180°C. Oil a large baking dish.

Heat the oil in a large skillet over low heat. Add the onions and cook for 10 minutes, or until soft and golden. Remove with a slotted spoon and set aside.

Increase the heat to high, add the beef, and cook, stirring, for 2–3 minutes, or until browned on all sides. Reduce the heat to medium, add the spices and salt and pepper to taste, and cook, stirring constantly, for 2 minutes.

Warm each tortilla in a lightly oiled nonstick skillet for 15 seconds on each side, then dip each, in turn, in the sauce. Top with a little of the beef, onions, and grated cheese and roll up.

Place seam-side down in the prepared baking dish, top with the remaining sauce and grated cheese, and bake in the preheated oven for 30 minutes. Serve at once.

ropa vieja

ingredients

SERVES 6

3 lb 5 oz/1½ kg flank beef
   steak or other stewing meat
beef stock
1 carrot, sliced
10 garlic cloves, sliced
salt and pepper
2 tbsp. vegetable oil
2 onions, thinly sliced
3–4 mild fresh green chilies,
   such as Anaheim or
   poblano, seeded and sliced
warmed flour tortillas (see
   page 206), to serve

salad garnishes

3 ripe tomatoes, diced
8–10 radishes, diced
3–4 tbsp. chopped fresh
   cilantro
4–5 scallions, chopped
1–2 limes, cut into wedges

method

Place the meat in a large pan and cover with a mixture of stock and water. Add the carrot and half the garlic with salt and pepper to taste. Cover and bring to a boil, then reduce the heat to low. Skim the scum that rises to the surface, then re-cover the pan and cook the meat gently for 2 hours, or until very tender.

Remove the pan from the heat and let the meat cool in the liquid. When cool enough to handle, remove from the liquid and shred with your fingers and a fork.

Heat the oil in a large, heavy-bottomed skillet. Add the remaining garlic, onions, and chilies and cook until lightly colored. Remove from the skillet and set aside.

Add the meat to the skillet and cook over medium–high heat until browned and crisp. Transfer to a serving dish. Top with the onion mixture and surround with the tomatoes, radishes, cilantro, scallions, and lime wedges. Serve with warmed tortillas.

spicy meat & chipotle hash

ingredients

SERVES 6

1 tbsp. vegetable oil

1 onion, finely chopped

1 lb/450 g leftover meat, such
as simmered pork or beef,
cooled and cut into strips

1 tbsp. mild chili powder

2 ripe tomatoes, seeded
and diced

about 8 fl oz/225 ml/ 1 cup
meat stock

1/2–1 canned chipotle chili,
mashed, plus a little of the
marinade, or a few shakes
of bottled chipotle salsa

chopped fresh cilantro, plus
extra to serve

to serve

warmed soft corn tortillas

4 fl oz/120 ml/1/2 cup sour
cream

4–6 tbsp. chopped radishes

3–4 crisp lettuce leaves, such
as romaine, shredded

method

Heat the oil in a skillet. Add the onion and cook until softened, stirring occasionally. Add the meat and cook for about 3 minutes, or until lightly browned, stirring.

Add the chili powder, tomatoes, and stock and cook until the tomatoes reduce to a sauce; mash the meat a little as it cooks.

Add the chili and continue to cook and mash until the sauce and meat are nearly blended.

Serve the dish, garnished with chopped cilantro, with a stack of warmed corn tortillas so that people can fill them with the meaty mixture to make tacos. Also serve sour cream, additional cilantro, radishes, and lettuce for each person to add to the meat.

meatballs in spicy-sweet sauce

ingredients

SERVES 4

8 oz/225 g ground pork
8 oz/225 g ground beef or lamb
6 tbsp. cooked rice or finely
     crushed tortillla chips
1 egg, lightly beaten
1¹/₂ onions, finely chopped
5 garlic cloves, finely chopped
¹/₂ tsp. ground cumin
large pinch of ground cinnamon
2 tbsp. raisins
1 tbsp. molasses sugar
1–2 tbsp. cider or wine vinegar
14 oz/400 g canned tomatoes,
     drained and chopped
12 fl oz/350 ml/1¹/₂ cups
     beef stock
1–2 tbsp. mild chili or ancho
     chili powder
1 tbsp. paprika
1 tbsp. chopped fresh cilantro
1 tbsp. chopped fresh parsley
2 tbsp. vegetable oil
2 sweet potatoes, peeled and
     cut into small chunks
salt and pepper
grated cheese, to serve

method

Mix the meat thoroughly with the rice or crushed tortilla chips, the egg, half the onion and garlic, the cumin, cinnamon, and raisins.

Divide the mixture into even-size pieces and roll into balls. Fry the balls in a nonstick skillet over medium heat until brown. Remove the balls from the skillet and set aside. Wipe the skillet clean.

Place the sugar in a food processor or blender with the vinegar, tomatoes, stock, chili powder, paprika, and remaining onion and garlic. Process until blended, then stir in the herbs. Set aside.

Heat the oil in the cleaned skillet. Add the sweet potatoes and cook until tender and golden brown. Pour in the blended sauce and add the meatballs to the skillet. Cook for 10 minutes, or until the meatballs are heated through and the flavors have combined. Season to taste with salt and pepper. Serve with grated cheese.

chili verde

ingredients

SERVES 4

2 lb 4 oz/1 kg pork, cut into
   bite-size chunks

1 onion, chopped

2 bay leaves

1 whole garlic bulb, cut in half

1 bouillon cube

2 garlic cloves, chopped

1 lb oz/450 g fresh tomatillos,
   husks removed, cooked in
   a small amount of water
   until just tender, then
   chopped, or canned

2 large fresh mild green chilies,
   such as Anaheim, or
   1 green bell pepper and
   2 jalapeño chilies, seeded
   and chopped

3 tbsp. vegetable oil

8 fl oz/225 ml/1 cup pork or
   chicken stock

$1/2$ tsp. mild chili powder, such
   as ancho or New Mexico

$1/2$ tsp. ground cumin

4–6 tbsp. chopped fresh
   cilantro, to garnish

to serve

warmed flour tortillas (see
   page 206)

lime wedges

method

Place the pork in a large, flameproof casserole with the onion, bay leaves, and garlic bulb. Add water to cover and the bouillon cube and bring to a boil. Skim off the scum that rises to the surface, reduce the heat to very low, and simmer gently for $1 1/2$ hours, or until the meat is very tender.

Meanwhile, place the chopped garlic in a food processor or blender with the tomatillos, chilies, and green bell pepper, if using. Process to a purée.

Heat the oil in a deep skillet. Add the tomatillo mixture and cook over medium–high heat for 10 minutes, or until thickened. Add the stock, chili powder, and cumin.

When the meat is tender, remove from the casserole and add to the sauce. Simmer gently for 20 minutes, or until the flavors are combined.

Garnish with the chopped cilantro and serve with warmed tortillas and lime wedges.

mole of pork & red chilies

ingredients

SERVES 6

2 lb 12 oz/1¼ kg pork
    shoulder or lean belly, cut
    into bite-size pieces

1 onion, chopped

1 whole garlic bulb

2 bay leaves

salt and pepper

1–2 bouillon cubes

6 dried ancho chilies

6 guajillo chilies or, if
    unavailable, de agua chilies

3–5 large ripe flavorful tomatoes

¼ tsp. ground cloves

¼ tsp. ground allspice

3 oz/80 g/¾ cup sesame
    seeds, toasted

1 large ripe plantain or
    banana, peeled and diced

3 tbsp. vegetable oil

6–8 waxy potatoes, cut into
    chunks

3 tbsp. yerba santa or, if
    unavailable, a combination
    of chopped fresh mint,
    oregano, and cilantro, plus
    a sprig to garnish

1 cinnamon stick

method

Place the pork in a large flameproof casserole with the onion, garlic, bay leaves, and salt and pepper to taste. Fill with cold water to the top. Bring to a boil, then reduce the heat to a slow simmer. Skim off the scum that rises to the surface, then stir in the bouillon cubes. Cook, covered, for 3 hours, or until the pork is very tender.

Meanwhile, lightly roast the chilies in an unoiled heavy-bottom skillet until they just change color. Place them in a heatproof bowl and cover with boiling water. Cover and let soften for 20–30 minutes.

Preheat the broiler to medium. Roast the tomatoes in the skillet to brown the bottoms, then char the tops under the hot broiler. Let cool.

When the chilies are softened, remove the stalks and seeds, transfer to a food processor or blender, and process with enough liquid to form a paste. Add the roasted tomatoes, cloves, allspice, two-thirds of the sesame seeds, and the plantain and process until smooth.

Remove the pork from the pan and reserve. Skim the fat from the surface of the stock.

Heat the oil in a separate pan. Add the tomato mixture and cook for 10 minutes, or until thickened. Add the potatoes and herbs with enough stock to keep the potatoes covered in sauce. Add the cinnamon stick. Cook, covered, until the potatoes are tender. Add the pork and heat through. Serve in bowls, sprinkled with the remaining sesame seeds.

spicy pork & vegetable hotpot

ingredients

SERVES 4

all-purpose flour, for coating

1 lb/450 g boneless pork, cut
   into 1-inch/2.5-cm cubes

1 tbsp. vegetable oil

8 oz/225 g chorizo sausage,
   outer casing removed, cut
   into bite-size chunks

1 onion, coarsely chopped

4 garlic cloves, finely chopped

2 celery stalks, chopped

1 cinnamon stick, broken

2 bay leaves

2 tsp. allspice

2 carrots, sliced

2–3 fresh red chilies, seeded
   and finely chopped

6 ripe tomatoes, peeled and
   chopped

1³/₄ pints/1 litre/4 cups pork
   or vegetable stock

2 sweet potatoes, cut into
   chunks

corn kernels, cut from 1 ear
   fresh corn

1 tbsp. chopped fresh oregano

salt and pepper

fresh oregano, to garnish

method

Season the flour well with salt and pepper and toss the
pork in it to coat. Heat the oil in a large, heavy-bottom
pan or ovenproof casserole. Add the chorizo and lightly
brown on all sides. Remove the chorizo with a slotted
spoon and set aside.

Add the pork, in batches, and cook until browned on all
sides. Remove the pork with a slotted spoon and set aside.
Add the onion, garlic, and celery to the pan and cook for
5 minutes, or until softened.

Add the cinnamon, bay leaves, and allspice and cook,
stirring, for 2 minutes. Add the pork, carrots, chilies,
tomatoes, and stock. Bring to a boil, then reduce the
heat, cover, and let simmer for 1 hour, or until the pork
is tender.

Return the chorizo to the pan with the sweet potatoes, corn,
oregano, and salt and pepper to taste. Cover and let simmer
for an additional 30 minutes, or until the vegetables are
tender. Serve garnished with oregano.

carnitas

ingredients

SERVES 4–6

2 lb 4 oz/1 kg pork,
    such as lean belly
1 onion, chopped
1 whole garlic bulb,
    cut in half
$1/2$ tsp. ground cumin
2 meat bouillon cubes
2 bay leaves
salt and pepper
fresh chili strips, to garnish

to serve

freshly cooked rice
refried beans (see page 202)
    or canned
salsa of your choice

method

Place the pork in a heavy-bottomed pan with the onion, garlic, cumin, bouillon cubes, and bay leaves. Add water to cover. Bring to a boil, then reduce the heat to very low. Skim off the scum that rises to the surface.

Continue to cook very gently for 2 hours, or until the pork is tender. Remove from the heat and let the pork cool in the liquid.

Remove the pork from the pan with a slotted spoon. Cut off any skin (roast separately to make crackling). Cut the pork into bite-size pieces and sprinkle with salt and pepper to taste. Reserve $1^1/4$ cups of the cooking liquid.

Brown the pork in a heavy-bottomed skillet for 15 minutes, to cook out the fat. Add the reserved cooking liquid and allow to reduce down. Continue to cook the meat for 15 minutes, covering the skillet to avoid splattering. Turn the pork every now and again.

Transfer the pork to a serving dish, garnish with chili strips, and serve with rice, refried beans, and salsa.

spicy pork with prunes

ingredients

SERVES 4–6

1 pork joint, such as leg
or shoulder, weighing
3 lb 5 oz/1.5 kg
juice of 2–3 limes
10 garlic cloves, chopped
3–4 tbsp. mild chili powder,
such as ancho or
New Mexico
4 tbsp. vegetable oil
salt
2 onions, chopped
18 fl oz/500 ml/2¼ cups
chicken stock
25 small tart tomatoes,
coarsely chopped
25 prunes, pitted
1–2 tsp. sugar
pinch of ground cinnamon
pinch of ground allspice
pinch of ground cumin
warmed corn tortillas, to serve

method

Combine the pork with the lime juice, garlic, chili powder, half the oil, and salt to taste in a nonmetallic bowl or dish. Cover and let marinate in the refrigerator overnight.

Preheat the oven to 350°F/180°C. Remove the pork from the marinade. Wipe the pork dry with paper towels and reserve the marinade. Heat the remaining oil in a flameproof casserole and brown the pork evenly until just golden. Add the onions, the reserved marinade, and stock. Cover and cook in the oven for 2–3 hours, or until tender.

Remove the casserole from the oven and spoon off the fat from the surface of the cooking liquid. Add the tomatoes. Return to the oven for 20 minutes, or until the tomatoes are tender. Remove the casserole from the oven. Mash the tomatoes into a coarse purée. Add the prunes and sugar, then adjust the seasoning, adding cinnamon, allspice, and cumin, as well as extra chili powder, if wished.

Increase the oven temperature to 400°F/200°C and return the casserole to the oven for an additional 20–30 minutes, or until the meat has browned on top and the juices have thickened.

Remove the meat from the casserole and let stand for a few minutes. Carefully carve the joint into thin slices and spoon the sauce over the top. Serve warm, with corn tortillas.

pork tostadas

ingredients

SERVES 6–8

1 tbsp. vegetable oil, plus
　　extra for cooking
1 small onion, finely chopped
2 garlic cloves, finely chopped
1 lb/450 g fresh ground pork
2 tsp. ground cumin
2 tsp. chili powder, plus
　　extra to garnish
1 tsp. ground cinnamon
salt and pepper
6 soft corn tortillas,
　　cut into wedges

to serve

shredded iceberg lettuce
sour cream
finely diced red bell pepper

method

Heat 1 tablespoon of oil in a heavy-bottom skillet over medium heat. Add the onion and garlic and cook, stirring frequently, for 5 minutes, or until softened. Increase the heat, add the ground pork, and cook, stirring constantly to break up any lumps, until well browned.

Add the cumin, chili powder, cinnamon, and salt and pepper to taste and cook, stirring, for 2 minutes. Cover and cook over low heat, stirring occasionally, for 10 minutes.

Meanwhile, heat a little oil in a nonstick skillet. Add the tortilla wedges, in batches, and cook on both sides until crisp. Drain on paper towels.

Transfer to a serving plate and top with the pork mixture, followed by the lettuce, a little sour cream, and diced bell pepper. Garnish with a sprinkling of chili powder and serve at once.

pork quesadillas with pinto beans

ingredients

SERVES 4

1 quantity Carnitas or about
   3^1/$_2$ oz/100 g cooked pork
   strips per person
1 ripe tomato, seeded
   and diced
^{1}/$_2$ onion, chopped
3 tbsp. chopped fresh cilantro
4 large flour tortillas
12 oz/350 g grated or thinly
   sliced cheese, such as
   mozzarella or Swiss
about 13^1/$_2$ oz/375 g/2 cups
   cooked drained pinto
   beans
hot salsa of your choice or
   bottled hot sauce, to taste
pickled jalapeño chilies, cut
   into thin rings, to taste
vegetable oil, for frying

to serve
pickled chilies
mixed salad

method

Heat the Carnitas in a pan and keep hot over low heat.

Combine the tomato, onion, and cilantro in a bowl and set aside.

Heat a tortilla in an unoiled nonstick skillet. Sprinkle the tortilla with cheese, then top with some of the meat, beans, and reserved tomato mixture. Add salsa and chili rings to taste. Fold over the sides of the tortilla to make a pocket.

Heat the pockets gently on each side in the skillet, adding a few drops of oil to keep it all supple and succulent, until the tortilla is golden and the cheese inside has melted. Keep warm. Repeat with the remaining tortillas and filling.

Transfer the quesadillas to a plate and serve at once with pickled chilies and salad.

chorizo & cheese quesadillas

ingredients

SERVES 4

4 oz/115 g mozzarella
   cheese, grated
4 oz/115 g Cheddar cheese,
   grated
8 oz/225 g cooked chorizo
   sausage, outer casing
   removed, or ham, diced
4 scallions, finely chopped
2 fresh green chilies, such
   as poblano, seeded and
   finely chopped
salt and pepper
8 flour tortillas (see page 206)
vegetable oil, for brushing
lime wedges, to garnish

method

Place the cheeses, chorizo, scallions, chilies, and salt and pepper to taste in a bowl and mix together.

Divide the mixture between 4 flour tortillas, then top with the remaining tortillas.

Brush a large, nonstick or heavy-bottom skillet with oil and heat over medium heat. Add 1 quesadilla and cook, pressing it down with a spatula, for 4–5 minutes, or until the underside is crisp and lightly browned. Turn over and cook the other side until the cheese is melting. Remove from the skillet and keep warm. Cook the remaining quesadillas individually.

Cut each quesadilla into quarters, arrange on a warmed serving plate, and serve, garnished with lime wedges.

burritos of lamb & black beans

ingredients

SERVES 4

1 lb 7 oz/650 g lean lamb

3 garlic cloves, finely chopped

juice of 1/2 lime

1/2 tsp. mild chili powder

1/2 tsp. ground cumin

large pinch of dried oregano
leaves, crushed

1–2 tbsp. extra-virgin olive oil

salt and pepper

14 oz/400 g/2 1/2 cups cooked
black beans, seasoned with
a little cumin, salt, and
pepper

4 large flour tortillas

2–3 tbsp. chopped fresh
cilantro, plus a few sprigs
to garnish

salsa, preferably Chipotle Salsa
(see page 164)

lime wedges, to serve
(optional)

method

Slice the lamb into thin strips, then combine with the garlic, lime juice, chili powder, cumin, oregano, and oil in a nonmetallic bowl. Season to taste with salt and pepper. Cover and let marinate in the refrigerator for 4 hours.

Warm the black beans with a little water in a pan.

Heat the tortillas in an unoiled nonstick skillet, sprinkling them with a few drops of water as they heat; wrap the tortillas in foil or a clean dish towel as you work to keep them warm. Alternatively, heat through in a stack in the skillet, moving the tortillas from the top to the bottom so that they warm evenly. Wrap to keep warm.

Stir-fry the lamb in a heavy-bottomed nonstick skillet over high heat until browned on all sides. Remove the skillet from the heat.

Spoon some of the beans and browned meat into a tortilla, sprinkle with cilantro, then add a little salsa and fold in the sides. Repeat with the remaining tortillas. Garnish with cilantro sprigs and serve at once with lime wedges and any spare salsa, if wished.

turkey with mole

ingredients

SERVES 4

4 turkey portions, each cut
   into 4 pieces
about 16 fl oz/450 ml/2 cups
   chicken stock, plus extra
   for thinning
about 8 fl oz/225 ml/1 cup
   water
1 onion, chopped
1 whole garlic bulb, divided
   into cloves and peeled
1 celery stalk, chopped
1 bay leaf
1 bunch fresh cilantro, finely
   chopped
18 fl oz/500 ml/2 1/4 cups mole
   poblano (see page 158) or
   use ready-made mole
   paste, thinned as
   instructed on the container
4–5 tbsp. sesame seeds,
   to garnish

method

Preheat the oven to 375°F/190°C. Arrange the turkey in
a large flameproof casserole. Pour the stock and water
around the turkey, then add the onion, garlic, celery, bay
leaf, and half the cilantro.

Cover and bake in the preheated oven for 1–1 1/2 hours,
or until the turkey is very tender. Add extra liquid if needed.

Warm the mole sauce in a pan with enough stock to
make it the consistency of thin cream.

To toast the sesame seeds for the garnish, place the seeds
in an unoiled skillet and dry-fry, shaking the skillet, until
lightly golden.

Arrange the turkey pieces on a serving plate and spoon
the warmed mole sauce over the top. Sprinkle with the
toasted sesame seeds and the remaining chopped
cilantro and serve.

chicken with yucatan vinegar sauce

ingredients

SERVES 4–6

8 small boned chicken thighs

chicken stock

15–20 garlic cloves, unpeeled

1 tsp. coarsely ground black pepper

1/2 tsp. ground cloves

2 tsp. crumbled dried oregano or 1/2 tsp. crushed bay leaves

about 1/2 tsp. salt

1 tbsp. lime juice

1 tsp. cumin seeds, lightly toasted

1 tbsp. all-purpose flour, plus extra for dredging

4 fl oz/120 ml/1 cup vegetable oil

3–4 onions, thinly sliced

2 fresh chilies, preferably mild yellow ones, such as Mexican Guero or similar Turkish or Greek chilies, seeded and sliced

3 1/2 fl oz/100 ml/scant 1/2 cup cider or sherry vinegar

method

Place the chicken in a pan with enough stock to cover. Bring to a boil, then reduce the heat and simmer for 5 minutes. Remove from the heat and let the chicken continue to cook while cooling in the stock.

Meanwhile, roast the garlic in an unoiled heavy-bottomed, nonstick skillet until the cloves are lightly browned on all sides and tender inside. Remove from the heat. When cool enough to handle, squeeze the flesh from the skins and place in a bowl.

Using a pestle and mortar, grind the garlic with the pepper, cloves, oregano, salt, lime juice, and three-quarters of the cumin seeds. Mix with the flour.

Remove the chicken from the stock, reserving the stock, and pat dry. Rub with two-thirds of the spice paste. Cover and let stand at room temperature for at least 30 minutes or overnight in the refrigerator.

Heat a little of the oil in a skillet and cook the onions and chilies until golden brown and softened. Pour in the vinegar and remaining cumin seeds, cook for a few minutes, then add the reserved stock and remaining spice paste. Boil, stirring, for 10 minutes, or until reduced in volume.

Dredge the chicken in flour. Heat the remaining oil in a heavy-bottomed skillet. Fry the chicken until lightly browned and the juices run clear when a skewer is inserted into the thickest part. Serve topped with the sauce.

chicken mole poblano

ingredients

SERVES 4

3 tbsp. olive oil

4 chicken pieces, about 6 oz/ 175 g each, halved

1 onion, chopped

2 garlic cloves, finely chopped

1 hot dried red chili, such as chipotle, or 2 milder dried chilies, such as ancho, reconstituted and finely chopped

1 tbsp. sesame seeds, toasted, plus extra to garnish

1 tbsp. chopped almonds

1/4 tsp. each of ground cinnamon, cumin, and cloves

3 tomatoes, peeled and chopped

2 tbsp. raisins

12 fl oz/350 ml/1 1/2 cups chicken stock

1 tbsp. peanut butter

1 oz/25 g semisweet chocolate with a high cocoa content, grated, plus extra to garnish

salt and pepper

method

Heat 2 tablespoons of the oil in a large skillet. Add the chicken and cook until browned on all sides. Remove the chicken pieces with a slotted spoon and set aside.

Add the onion, garlic, and chilies and cook for 5 minutes, or until softened. Add the sesame seeds, almonds, and spices and cook, stirring, for 2 minutes. Add the tomatoes, raisins, stock, peanut butter, and chocolate and stir well. Season to taste with salt and pepper and let simmer for 5 minutes.

Transfer the mixture to a food processor or blender and process until smooth (you may need to do this in batches).

Return the mixture to the skillet, add the chicken, and bring to a boil. Reduce the heat, cover, and let simmer for 1 hour, or until the chicken is very tender, adding more liquid if necessary.

Serve garnished with sesame seeds and a little grated chocolate.

tequila-marinated crisp chicken wings

ingredients

SERVES 4

2 lb/900 g chicken wings

11 garlic cloves, finely chopped

juice of 2 limes

juice of 1 orange

2 tbsp. tequila

1 tbsp. mild chili powder

2 tsp. Chipotle Salsa
   (see page 164) or
   2 dried chipotle chilies,
   reconstituted and puréed

2 tbsp. vegetable oil

1 tsp. sugar

$1/4$ tsp. ground allspice

pinch of ground cinnamon

pinch of ground cumin

pinch of dried oregano

grilled or broiled tomato
   halves, to serve (optional)

method

Cut the chicken wings into 2 pieces at the joint.

Place the chicken wings in a nonmetallic dish and add the remaining ingredients. Toss well to coat, then cover and let marinate in the refrigerator for at least 3 hours or overnight.

Preheat the grill. Cook the chicken wings over the hot coals of the grill for 15–20 minutes, or until crisply browned and the juices run clear when a skewer is inserted into the thickest part of the meat, turning occasionally. Alternatively, cook in a ridged grill pan. Serve at once, with grilled or broiled tomato halves, if wished.

green chili & chicken chilaquiles

ingredients

SERVES 4–6

12 stale tortillas, cut into strips
1 tbsp. vegetable oil
1 small cooked chicken, meat
    removed from the bones
    and cut into bite-size pieces
salsa verde
3 tbsp. chopped fresh cilantro
1 tsp. finely chopped fresh
    oregano or thyme
4 garlic cloves, finely chopped
1/4 tsp. ground cumin
12 oz/350 g/3 cups grated
    Cheddar, manchego,
    or mozzarella cheese
16 fl oz/450 ml/2 cups
    chicken stock
4 oz/115 g/1 1/2 cups freshly
    grated Parmesan cheese

to serve

12 fl oz /350 ml/1 1/2 cups
    sour cream
3–5 scallions, thinly sliced
pickled chilies

method

Preheat the oven to 375°F/190°C. Place the tortilla strips in a roasting pan, toss with the oil, and bake in the oven for 30 minutes, or until they are crisp and golden.

Arrange the chicken in a 9- x 13-inch/23- x 33-cm flameproof casserole, then sprinkle with half the salsa, cilantro, oregano, garlic, cumin, and some of the Cheddar, manchego, or mozzarella cheese. Repeat these layers and top with the tortilla strips.

Pour the stock over the top, then sprinkle with the remaining cheese.

Bake in the oven at the same temperature for 30 minutes, or until heated through and the cheese is lightly golden in areas.

Serve with a spoonful of sour cream, sliced scallions, and pickled chilies to taste.

chicken tostadas with green salsa & chipotle

ingredients

SERVES 4–6

6 soft corn tortillas

vegetable oil, for frying

1 lb/450 g skinned, boned
chicken breast or thigh, cut
into strips or small pieces

8 fl oz/225 ml/1 cup chicken
stock

2 garlic cloves, finely chopped

14 oz/400 g refried beans
(see page 202) or canned

large pinch of ground cumin

8 oz/225 g/2 cups grated
cheese

1 tbsp. chopped fresh cilantro

2 ripe tomatoes, diced

handful of crisp lettuce leaves,
such as romaine, shredded

4–6 radishes, diced

3 scallions, thinly sliced

1 ripe avocado, pitted,
peeled, diced or sliced,
and tossed with lime juice

sour cream, to taste

1–2 canned chipotle chilies in
adobo marinade

method

To make the tostadas, fry the tortillas in a small amount of oil in a nonstick skillet until crisp. Set aside.

Place the chicken in a pan with the stock and garlic. Bring to a boil, then reduce the heat and cook for 1–2 minutes, or until the chicken begins to turn opaque.

Remove the chicken from the heat and let stand in its hot liquid to cook through.

Heat the beans in a separate pan with enough water to form a smooth purée. Add the cumin and keep warm.

Reheat the tostadas under a preheated medium broiler, if necessary. Spread the hot beans on the tostadas, then sprinkle with the cheese. Lift the cooked chicken from the liquid and divide between the tostadas. Top with the cilantro, tomatoes, lettuce, radishes, scallions, avocado, sour cream, and a few strips of chipotle. Serve immediately.

chicken fajitas

ingredients

SERVES 4

3 tbsp. olive oil, plus
extra for drizzling
3 tbsp. maple syrup or honey
1 tbsp. red wine vinegar
2 garlic cloves, crushed
2 tsp. dried oregano
1–2 tsp. dried red pepper flakes
salt and pepper
4 skinless, boneless chicken
breasts
2 red bell peppers, seeded
and cut into 1-inch/
2.5-cm strips
8 flour tortillas (see page
206), warmed

method

Place the oil, maple syrup, vinegar, garlic, oregano, pepper flakes, and salt and pepper to taste in a large, shallow dish or bowl and mix together.

Slice the chicken across the grain into slices 1 inch/2.5 cm thick. Toss in the marinade until well coated. Cover and let chill in the refrigerator for 2–3 hours, turning occasionally.

Heat a grill pan until hot. Lift the chicken slices from the marinade with a slotted spoon, lay on the grill pan, and cook over medium-high heat for 3–4 minutes on each side, or until cooked through. Remove the chicken to a warmed serving plate and keep warm.

Add the bell peppers, skin-side down, to the grill pan and cook for 2 minutes on each side. Transfer to the serving plate.

Serve at once with the warmed tortillas to be used as wraps.

chicken tacos from puebla

ingredients

SERVES 4

8 soft corn tortillas

2 tsp. vegetable oil

8–12 oz/225–350 g leftover
   cooked chicken, diced or
   shredded

salt and pepper

8 oz/225 g canned refried
   beans, warmed with
   2 tbsp. water to thin

$1/4$ tsp. ground cumin

$1/4$ tsp. dried oregano

1 avocado, pitted, peeled,
   sliced, and tossed with
   lime juice

 salsa of your choice

1 canned chipotle chili in
   adobo marinade, chopped,
   or bottled chipotle salsa

6 fl oz/175 ml/$3/4$ cup sour
   cream

$1/2$ onion, chopped

handful of lettuce leaves

5 radishes, diced

method

Heat the tortillas through in an unoiled nonstick skillet in a stack, alternating the tortillas from the top to the bottom so that they warm evenly. Wrap in foil or a clean dish towel to keep them warm.

Heat the oil in a skillet. Add the chicken and heat through. Season to taste with salt and pepper.

Combine the warmed refried beans with the cumin and oregano.

Spread one tortilla with the refried beans, then top with a spoonful of the chicken, a slice or two of avocado, a little salsa, chipotle to taste, a spoonful of sour cream, and a sprinkling of onion, lettuce, and radishes. Season to taste with salt and pepper, then roll up as tightly as you can. Repeat with the remaining tortillas and serve at once.

fresh from the sea

The shape of Mexico is defined by its thousands of miles of coastline, and its cuisine is rich in the fruits of the sea – fish and shellfish. Swordfish, salmon, sea bass, red snapper, sole, and cod find their way onto the typical Mexican menu, as do squid, shrimp, scallops, and crab.

As with meat, seafood is given the spicy treatment and chilies add varying degrees of heat to enticing stews, fresh citrus marinades, flavorful pastes for coating the fish, innovative sauces with unusual ingredients like avocado and papaya, luscious fillings for tacos and burritos, and tasty toppings for tostadas. Refried beans are used in fish recipes in much the same way as they are in meat dishes – a tostada is quickly made by putting a layer of beans on top of a fried tortilla, adding chunks of poached white fish, and finishing with salsa and a spoonful of soured cream.

In some recipes, the fish is served "cured" rather than cooked – that is, it is left for several hours in a citrus marinade, and the acid from the fruit effectively cooks the flesh. If you are searching for a fish recipe that can be prepared well ahead of time and looks and tastes really impressive, then try the citrus-marinated fish or the ceviche salad at the end of this chapter.

fish with yucatan flavors

ingredients

SERVES 8

4 tbsp. annatto seeds, soaked
    in water overnight
3 garlic cloves, finely chopped
1 tbsp. mild chili powder
1 tbsp. paprika
1 tsp. ground cumin
$1/2$ tsp. dried oregano
2 tbsp. beer or tequila
juice of 1 lime and I orange or
    3 tbsp. pineapple juice
2 tbsp. olive oil
2 tbsp. chopped fresh cilantro
$1/4$ tsp. ground cinnamon
$1/4$ tsp. ground cloves
2 lb 4 oz/1 kg swordfish steaks
banana leaves, for wrapping
    (optional)
fresh cilantro sprigs,
    to garnish
orange wedges, to serve

method

Drain the annatto, then crush them to a paste with a pestle and mortar. Work in the garlic, chili powder, paprika, cumin, oregano, beer, fruit juice, oil, cilantro, cinnamon, and cloves.

Smear the paste on to the fish, cover, and marinate in the refrigerator for at least 3 hours or overnight.

Wrap the fish steaks in banana leaves, tying with string to make pockets. Bring enough water to a boil in a steamer, then add a batch of pockets to the top part of the steamer and steam for 15 minutes, or until the fish is cooked through.

Alternatively, cook the fish without wrapping in the banana leaves. To cook on the grill, place in a hinged basket, or on a rack, and cook over hot coals for 5–6 minutes on each side, or until cooked through. Or cook the fish under a preheated hot broiler for 5–6 minutes on each side, or until cooked through.

Garnish with cilantro sprigs and serve with orange wedges for squeezing over the fish.

spicy broiled salmon

ingredients

SERVES 4

4 salmon steaks, about
    6–8 oz/175–225 g each

marinade

4 garlic cloves

2 tbsp. extra-virgin olive oil

pinch of ground allspice

pinch of ground cinnamon

juice of 2 limes

1–2 tsp. marinade from
    canned chipotle chilies or
    bottled chipotle chili salsa

1/4 tsp. ground cumin

pinch of sugar

salt and pepper

lime slices, to garnish

to serve

tomato wedges

3 scallions, finely chopped

shredded lettuce

method

To make the marinade, finely chop the garlic and place in a nonmetallic bowl with the oil, allspice, cinnamon, lime juice, chipotle marinade, cumin, and sugar. Add salt and pepper to taste and stir to combine.

Coat the salmon with the garlic mixture, then transfer to a large nonmetallic dish. Cover with plastic wrap and let marinate in the refrigerator for 1 hour.

Preheat the broiler to medium. Transfer the salmon to a broiler pan and cook under the hot broiler for 3–4 minutes on each side, or until cooked through. Alternatively, cook the salmon over hot coals on a grill until cooked through.

To serve, mix the tomato wedges with the scallions. Place the salmon on individual plates and arrange the tomato salad and shredded lettuce alongside. Garnish with lime slices and serve immediately.

fish baked with lime

ingredients

SERVES 4

2 lb 4 oz/1 kg white fish
   fillets, such as bass,
   flounder, or cod

salt and pepper

1 lime, halved

3 tbsp. virgin olive oil

1 large onion, finely chopped

3 garlic cloves, finely chopped

2–3 pickled jalapeño chilies,
   chopped, plus extra whole
   chilies to serve (optional)

6–8 tbsp. chopped fresh
   cilantro

lemon and lime wedges,
   to serve

method

Preheat the oven to 350°F/180°C. Place the fish fillets in a nonmetallic bowl and sprinkle with salt and pepper to taste. Squeeze the juice from the lime over the fish.

Heat the oil in a skillet. Add the onion and garlic and cook for 2 minutes, or until softened, stirring frequently. Remove from the heat.

Place a third of the onion mixture and a little of the chilies and cilantro in the bottom of a shallow baking dish or roasting pan. Arrange the fish on top. Top with the remaining onion mixture, chilies, and cilantro.

Bake in the oven for 15–20 minutes, or until the fish has become slightly opaque and firm to the touch. Serve at once, with lemon and lime wedges for squeezing over the fish and whole pickled chilies, if wished.

fish fillets with papaya sauce

ingredients

SERVES 4

4 white fish fillets, such as
sea bass, sole, or cod,
about 6 oz/175 g each,
skinned
olive oil, for drizzling
juice of 1 lime
2 tbsp. chopped fresh cilantro
salt and pepper
lime wedges, to garnish

for the papaya sauce

1 large ripe papaya
1 tbsp. freshly squeezed
orange juice
1 tbsp. freshly squeezed
lime juice
1 tbsp. olive oil
1–2 tsp. Tabasco sauce

method

Preheat the oven to 350°F/180°C. Place the fish in a shallow ovenproof dish. Drizzle with oil and squeeze over the lime juice. Sprinkle the chopped cilantro over the fish and season to taste with salt and pepper.

Cover the dish tightly with foil and bake in the preheated oven for 15–20 minutes, or until the fish is just flaking.

Meanwhile, to make the sauce, halve the papaya and scoop out the seeds. Peel the halves and chop the flesh. Place the flesh in a food processor or blender and add the orange and lime juices, oil, and Tabasco to taste. Process until smooth.

Transfer the sauce to a pan and heat through gently for 3–4 minutes. Season to taste with salt and pepper.

Serve the fish fillets, in their cooking juices, with the sauce spooned over, garnished with lime wedges.

squid simmered with tomatoes & olives

ingredients

SERVES 4

3 tbsp. virgin olive oil

2 lb/900 g cleaned squid, cut into rings and tentacles

salt and pepper

1 onion, chopped

3 garlic cloves, chopped

14 oz/400 g canned chopped tomatoes

$1/2$–1 fresh mild to medium green chili, seeded and chopped

1 tbsp. finely chopped fresh parsley

$1/4$ tsp. chopped fresh thyme

$1/4$ tsp. chopped fresh oregano

$1/4$ tsp. chopped fresh marjoram

large pinch of ground cinnamon

large pinch of ground allspice

large pinch of sugar

15–20 pimiento-stuffed green olives, sliced

1 tbsp. capers

1 tbsp. chopped fresh cilantro, to garnish

method

Heat the oil in a deep, heavy-bottomed skillet. Add the squid and lightly cook until it turns opaque. Season to taste with salt and pepper and remove from the skillet with a slotted spoon. Set aside in a bowl.

Add the onion and garlic to the remaining oil in the skillet and cook for 5 minutes, or until softened. Stir in the tomatoes, chili, herbs, cinnamon, allspice, sugar, and olives. Cover and cook over medium–low heat for 5–10 minutes, or until the mixture thickens slightly. Uncover the skillet and cook for an additional 5 minutes to concentrate the flavors.

Stir in the reserved squid and any of the juices that have gathered in the bowl. Add the capers and heat through.

Adjust the seasoning, then serve immediately, garnished with cilantro.

southwestern seafood stew

ingredients

SERVES 4

1 each of yellow, red, and
  orange bell peppers,
  seeded and quartered

1 lb/450 g ripe tomatoes

2 large fresh mild green
  chilies, such as poblano

6 garlic cloves, peeled

2 tsp. dried oregano or dried
  mixed herbs

2 tbsp. olive oil, plus extra for
  drizzling

1 large onion, finely chopped

16 fl oz/450 ml/2 cups fish,
  vegetable, or chicken stock

1 lime, finely grated rind and
  juice of

2 tbsp. chopped fresh cilantro,
  plus extra to garnish

1 bay leaf

salt and pepper

1 lb/450 g red snapper fillets,
  skinned and cut into
  chunks

8 oz/225 g raw shrimp,
  shelled and deveined

8 oz/225 g cleaned squid,
  cut into rings

method

Preheat the oven to 400°F/200°C. Place the bell pepper
fourths, skin side up, in a roasting pan with the tomatoes,
chilies, and garlic. Sprinkle with the dried oregano and
drizzle with oil.

Roast in the preheated oven for 30 minutes, or until the
bell peppers are well browned and softened.

Remove the roasted vegetables from the oven and let
stand until cool enough to handle. Peel off the skins
from the bell peppers, tomatoes, and chilies and chop
the flesh. Finely chop the garlic.

Heat the oil in a large pan. Add the onion and cook
for 5 minutes, or until softened. Add the bell peppers,
tomatoes, chilies, garlic, stock, lime rind and juice,
chopped cilantro, bay leaf, and salt and pepper to taste.
Bring to a boil, then stir in the seafood. Reduce the
heat, cover, and let simmer gently for 10 minutes, or
until the seafood is just cooked through. Garnish with
chopped cilantro before serving.

pan-fried scallops mexicana

ingredients

SERVES 4

2 tbsp. butter

2 tbsp. virgin olive oil

1 lb 7 oz/650 g scallops, shelled

4–5 scallions, thinly sliced

3–4 garlic cloves, finely chopped

1/2 fresh green chili, seeded and finely chopped

2 tbsp. finely chopped fresh cilantro

1/2 lime

salt and pepper

lime wedges, to serve

method

Heat half the butter and oil in a large, heavy-bottomed skillet until the butter foams.

Add the scallops and cook quickly until just turning opaque; do not overcook. Remove from the skillet with a slotted spoon and keep warm.

Add the remaining butter and oil to the skillet, then toss in the scallions and garlic and cook over medium heat until the scallions are wilted. Return the scallops to the skillet.

Remove the skillet from the heat and add the chili and cilantro. Squeeze in the lime juice. Season to taste with salt and pepper and stir to mix well.

Serve immediately with lime wedges for squeezing over the scallops.

shrimp in green bean sauce

ingredients

SERVES 4

2 tbsp. vegetable oil

3 onions, chopped

5 garlic cloves, chopped

5–7 ripe tomatoes, diced

6–8 oz/175–225 g green beans,
    cut into 2-inch/5-cm pieces
    and blanched for 1 minute

1/4 tsp. ground cumin

pinch of ground allspice

pinch of ground cinnamon

1/2–1 canned chipotle chili in
    adobo marinade, with
    some of the marinade

16 fl oz/450 ml/2 cups fish
    stock or water mixed with
    1 fish bouillon cube

1 lb/450 g raw shrimp,
    shelled and deveined

fresh cilantro sprigs,
    to garnish

1 lime, cut into wedges,
    to serve (optional)

method

Heat the oil in a large, deep skillet. Add the onions and garlic and cook over low heat for 5–10 minutes, or until softened. Add the tomatoes and cook for an additional 2 minutes.

Add the green beans, cumin, allspice, cinnamon, the chili and marinade, and stock. Bring to a boil, then reduce the heat and simmer for a few minutes to combine the flavors.

Add the shrimp and cook for 1–2 minutes only, then remove the skillet from the heat and let the shrimp steep in the hot liquid to finish cooking. They are cooked when they have turned a bright pink color.

Serve the shrimp immediately, garnished with the cilantro sprigs and accompanied by the lime wedges, if wished.

chili-marinated shrimp with avocado sauce

ingredients

SERVES 4

1 lb 7 oz/650 g large raw
   shrimp, shelled, deveined,
   and tails left intact

1/2 tsp. ground cumin

1/2 tsp. mild chili powder

1/2 tsp. paprika

2 tbsp. orange juice

grated rind of 1 orange

2 tbsp. extra-virgin olive oil

2 tbsp. chopped fresh cilantro,
   plus extra to garnish

salt and pepper

2 ripe avocados

1/2 onion, finely chopped

1/4 fresh green or red chili,
   seeded and chopped

juice of 1/2 lime

method

Preheat the grill. Combine the shrimp with the cumin, chili powder, paprika, orange juice and rind, oil, and half the cilantro. Season to taste with salt and pepper.

Thread the shrimp on to metal skewers, or bamboo skewers that have been soaked in cold water for 30 minutes.

Cut the avocados in half around the pit. Twist apart, then remove the pit with a knife. Carefully peel off the skin, then dice the flesh. Immediately combine the avocados with the remaining cilantro, onion, chili, and lime juice in a nonmetallic bowl. Season to taste with salt and pepper and set aside.

Place the shrimp over the hot coals of the grill and cook for only a few minutes on each side, or until bright pink and opaque.

Serve the shrimp garnished with chopped cilantro and accompanied by the avocado sauce.

fish burritos

ingredients

SERVES 4–6

about 1 lb/450 g firm-fleshed
white fish, such as red
snapper or cod

salt and pepper

1/4 tsp. ground cumin

pinch of dried oregano

4 garlic cloves, finely chopped

4 fl oz/120 ml/1/2 cup fish
stock or water mixed with
1 fish bouillon cube

juice of 1/2 lemon or lime

8 flour tortillas

2–3 romaine lettuce leaves,
shredded

2 ripe tomatoes, diced

1 quantity salsa cruda (see
page 168)

lemon slices, to serve

method

Season the fish to taste with salt and pepper, then place in a pan with the cumin, oregano, garlic, and enough stock to cover.

Bring to a boil, then cook for 1 minute. Remove the pan from the heat. Let the fish cool in the cooking liquid for 30 minutes.

Remove the fish from the liquid with a slotted spoon and break up into bite-size pieces. Place in a nonmetallic bowl, sprinkle with the lemon juice, and set aside.

Heat the tortillas in an unoiled nonstick skillet, sprinkling them with a few drops of water as they heat; wrap the tortillas in foil or a clean dish towel as you work to keep them warm.

Arrange shredded lettuce in the center of one tortilla, spoon on a few big chunks of the fish, then sprinkle with the tomatoes. Add some of the Salsa Cruda. Repeat with the other tortillas and serve at once with lemon slices.

fish tacos ensenada-style

ingredients

SERVES 4

about 1 lb/450 g firm-fleshed
   white fish, such as red
   snapper or cod
$1/4$ tsp. dried oregano
$1/4$ tsp. ground cumin
1 tsp. mild chili powder
2 garlic cloves, finely chopped
salt and pepper
3 tbsp. all-purpose flour
vegetable oil, for frying
$1/4$ red cabbage, thinly sliced
   or shredded
juice of 2 limes
hot pepper sauce or salsa,
   to taste
8 corn tortillas (see page 206)
1 tbsp. chopped fresh cilantro
$1/2$ onion, chopped (optional)
salsa of your choice

method

Place the fish on a plate and sprinkle with half the oregano, cumin, chili powder, and garlic, and salt and pepper to taste. Dust with the flour.

Heat the oil in a skillet until it is smoking, then fry the fish in several batches until it is golden on the outside and just tender in the middle. Remove from the skillet and place on paper towels to drain.

In a nonmetallic bowl, combine the cabbage with the remaining oregano, cumin, chili powder, and garlic, then stir in the lime juice and salt and hot pepper sauce to taste. Set aside.

Heat the tortillas in an unoiled nonstick skillet, sprinkling with a few drops of water as they heat; wrap the tortillas in foil or a clean dish towel as you work to keep them warm. Alternatively, heat through in a stack in the skillet, alternating the tortillas from the top to the bottom so that they warm evenly.

Place some of the warm fried fish in each tortilla with a large spoonful of the hot cabbage salad. Sprinkle with cilantro and onion, if using. Add some salsa and serve immediately.

fish & refried bean tostadas with green salsa

ingredients

SERVES 4

about 1 lb/450 g firm-fleshed
white fish, such as red
snapper or cod
4 fl oz/120 ml/½ cup fish stock
¼ tsp. ground cumin
¼ tsp. mild chili powder
pinch of dried oregano
4 garlic cloves, finely chopped
salt and pepper
juice of ½ lemon or lime
8 soft corn tortillas
vegetable oil, for frying
14 oz/400 g canned refried
beans, warmed with 2 tbsp.
water to thin
salsa of your choice
2–3 romaine lettuce leaves,
shredded
3 tbsp. chopped fresh cilantro
2 tbsp. chopped onion

to garnish
sour cream
chopped fresh herbs

method

Place the fish in a pan with the stock, cumin, chili powder, oregano, garlic, and salt and pepper to taste. Stir and gently bring to a boil, then immediately remove the pan from the heat. Let the fish cool in the cooking liquid.

When cool enough to handle, remove the fish from the liquid with a slotted spoon; reserve the cooking liquid. Break the fish up into bite-size pieces, place in a nonmetallic bowl, sprinkle with the lemon juice, and set aside until required.

To make the tostadas, fry the tortillas in a small amount of oil in a nonstick skillet until crisp. Spread the tostadas evenly with the warmed refried beans.

Gently reheat the fish with a little of the reserved cooking liquid in a pan, then spoon the fish on top of the beans. Top each tostada with some of the salsa, lettuce, cilantro, and onion. Garnish each one with a generous spoonful of sour cream and a sprinkling of chopped fresh herbs. Serve the tostadas immediately.

chili-shrimp tacos

ingredients

SERVES 4

1 lb 5 oz/600 g raw shrimp, shelled and deveined

2 tbsp. chopped fresh flatleaf parsley

12 tortilla shells

scallions, chopped, to garnish

for the taco sauce

1 tbsp. olive oil

1 onion, finely chopped

1 green bell pepper, seeded and diced

1–2 fresh hot green chilies, such as jalapeño, seeded and finely chopped

3 garlic cloves, crushed

1 tsp. ground cumin

1 tsp. ground coriander

1 tsp. brown sugar

1 lb/450 g ripe tomatoes, peeled and coarsely chopped

juice of $1/2$ lemon

salt and pepper

to serve

sour cream

method

Preheat the oven to 350°F/180°C. To make the sauce, heat the oil in a deep skillet over medium heat. Add the onion and cook for 5 minutes, or until softened. Add the bell pepper and chilies and cook for 5 minutes. Add the garlic, cumin, coriander, and sugar and cook the sauce for an additional 2 minutes, stirring.

Add the tomatoes, lemon juice, and salt and pepper to taste. Bring to a boil, then reduce the heat and let simmer for 10 minutes.

Stir in the shrimp and parsley, cover, and cook gently for 5–8 minutes, or until the shrimp are pink and tender.

Meanwhile, place the tortilla shells, open-side down, on a baking sheet. Warm in the preheated oven for 2–3 minutes.

To serve, spoon the shrimp mixture into the tortilla shells and top with a spoonful of sour cream.

crab & avocado soft tacos

ingredients

SERVES 4

8 soft corn tortillas

1 avocado

lime or lemon juice, for tossing

4–6 tbsp. sour cream

9–10 oz/250–280 g cooked
  crabmeat

$1/2$ lime

$1/2$ fresh green chili, such as
  jalapeño or serrano,
  seeded and chopped or
  thinly sliced

1 ripe tomato, seeded
  and diced

$1/2$ small onion, finely chopped

2 tbsp. chopped fresh cilantro

salsa of your choice, to serve
  (optional)

method

Heat the tortillas in an unoiled nonstick skillet, sprinkling them with a few drops of water as they heat; wrap in foil or a clean dish towel as you work to keep them warm.

Cut the avocado in half around the pit. Twist apart, then remove the pit with a knife. Carefully peel off the skin from the avocado, slice the flesh, and toss in lime juice to prevent discoloration.

Spread one tortilla with sour cream. Top with crabmeat, a squeeze of lime, and a sprinkling of chili, tomato, onion, cilantro, and avocado, adding a generous spoonful of salsa, if desired. Fold in the sides to form a cornet, repeat with the remaining tortillas, and serve at once.

salpicon of crab

ingredients

SERVES 4

$1/4$ red onion, chopped

$1/2$–1 fresh green chili, seeded
and chopped

juice of $1/2$ lime

1 tbsp. cider or other fruit
vinegar, such as raspberry

1 tbsp. chopped fresh cilantro

1 tbsp. extra-virgin olive oil

8–12 oz/225–350 g fresh
crabmeat

lettuce leaves, to serve

to garnish

1 avocado

lime juice, for tossing

1–2 ripe tomatoes

3–5 radishes

method

In a large, nonmetallic bowl, combine the red onion with the chili, lime juice, vinegar, cilantro, and oil. Add the crabmeat and toss the ingredients lightly together.

To make the garnish, cut the avocado in half around the pit. Twist apart, then remove the pit with a knife. Carefully peel off the skin and slice the flesh. Toss the avocado gently in lime juice to prevent discoloration.

Halve the tomatoes, then remove the cores and seeds. Dice the flesh. Thinly slice the radishes.

Arrange the crab salad on a bed of lettuce leaves and garnish with the avocado, tomatoes, and radishes. Serve at once.

citrus-marinated fish

ingredients

SERVES 4

1 lb/450 g white-fleshed fish
   fillets, cut into bite-size
   chunks

juice of 6–8 limes

2–3 ripe flavorful tomatoes,
   diced

3 fresh green chilies, such as
   jalapeño or serrano,
   seeded and thinly sliced

$1/2$ tsp. dried oregano

$1/3$ cup extra-virgin olive oil

1 small onion, finely chopped

salt and pepper

2 tbsp. chopped fresh cilantro

method

Place the fish in a nonmetallic dish, add the lime juice, and mix well. Cover and let chill in the refrigerator for 5 hours, or until the fish looks opaque. (Do not leave too long, otherwise the texture will spoil.) Turn from time to time so that the lime juice permeates the fish.

An hour before serving, add the tomatoes, chilies, oregano, oil, and onion. Season to taste with salt and pepper. Return to the refrigerator.

About 15 minutes before serving, remove from the refrigerator so that the oil comes to room temperature. Serve sprinkled with cilantro.

ceviche salad

ingredients

SERVES 4

1 lb/450 g salmon, red snapper,
   or sole fillets, skinned and
   cut into strips or slices
1 small onion, finely chopped
1 fresh jalapeño chili or 2 small
   fresh mild green chilies,
   seeded and finely chopped
juice of 3 limes
1 tbsp. extra-virgin olive oil
1 tbsp. chopped fresh cilantro,
   plus extra to garnish
1 tbsp. snipped fresh chives
   or dill
salt and pepper
2 tomatoes, peeled and diced
shredded crisp lettuce.
2 tbsp. capers, rinsed
   (optional)

method

Place the fish, onion, chili, lime juice, oil, and herbs in a
nonmetallic dish and mix together. Cover and let chill in
the refrigerator for 8 hours or overnight, stirring occasionally
to ensure that the fish is well coated in the marinade.

When ready to serve, remove the dish from the refrigerator
and season to taste with salt and pepper.

Arrange the fish mixture on top of shredded crisp lettuce
on a large serving plate. Sprinkle the capers over the
mixture, and sprinkle with chopped cilantro to garnish.

on the side

The Mexicans really know how to spice things up a bit, as you will discover in this chapter. There are recipes for the most amazing salsas, vegetables, and salads, as well as for rice dishes with a difference, and for cooking beans – including Mexico's famous "refried beans," which feature in many recipes.

Beans are a staple in Mexican cooking and in every marketplace café and home kitchen there will be a pot of simmering beans, ready to be added to a typical recipe or simply eaten from a bowl with a few tortillas. The types of beans used vary throughout the country, from the tender pale pink beans of the north, such as pinto, to the inky black beans of the south.

Salsas also appear on every table in every corner of Mexico – made of vegetables and fruits, raw, cooked, chopped, chunky, smooth, spicy, mild, or fiery, they add interest, color, texture, and flavor. Sauces have a similar role – do be sure to try Mole Poblano, the classic sauce of chilies and chocolate!

At the end of this chapter you will find a recipe for flour tortillas, the thin, pancake-like flat breads. They are remarkably easy to make and will bring a special touch of authenticity to your Mexican menu.

black bean nachos

ingredients

SERVES 4

8 oz/225 g/1 cup dried black
  beans, or canned black
  beans, drained

6–8 oz/175–225 g/1$\frac{1}{2}$–2
  cups grated cheese, such
  as Cheddar, fontina,
  romano, Asiago, or a
  combination

about $\frac{1}{4}$ tsp. cumin seeds or
  ground cumin

about 4 tbsp. sour cream

thinly sliced pickled jalapeño
  chilies (optional)

1 tbsp. chopped fresh cilantro

handful of shredded lettuce

tortilla chips, to serve

method

If using dried black beans, soak the beans overnight,
then drain. Put into a pan, cover with water, and bring to
a boil. Boil for 10 minutes, then reduce the heat and
simmer for 1$\frac{1}{2}$ hours, or until tender. Drain well.

Preheat the oven to 375°F/190°C. Spread the beans in
a shallow ovenproof dish, then scatter the cheese over
the top. Sprinkle with cumin to taste.

Bake in the preheated oven for 10–15 minutes, or until
the beans are cooked through and the cheese is bubbly
and melted.

Remove from the oven and spoon the sour cream on
top. Add the chilies, if using, and sprinkle with cilantro
and lettuce.

Arrange the tortilla chips around the beans, placing
them in the mixture. Serve the nachos at once.

guacamole

ingredients

SERVES 4

2 large, ripe avocados
juice of 1 lime, or to taste
2 tsp. olive oil
1/2 onion, finely chopped
1 fresh green chili, such as
    poblano, seeded and
    finely chopped
1 garlic clove, crushed
1/4 tsp. ground cumin
1 tbsp. chopped fresh
    cilantro, plus extra to
    garnish (optional)
salt and pepper

method

Cut the avocados in half lengthwise and twist the 2 halves in opposite directions to separate. Stab the pit with the point of a sharp knife and lift out.

Peel, then coarsely chop the avocado halves and place in a nonmetallic bowl. Squeeze over the lime juice and add the oil.

Mash the avocados with a fork until the desired consistency—either chunky or smooth. Blend in the onion, chili, garlic, cumin, and chopped cilantro, then season to taste with salt and pepper.

Transfer to a serving dish and serve at once, to avoid discoloration, sprinkled with extra chopped cilantro, if liked.

cilantro mayonnaise

ingredients

SERVES 4

1 egg

2 tsp. prepared mustard

1/2 tsp. salt

squeeze of lemon juice

2 tbsp. chopped fresh cilantro

1 fresh mild green chili,
   seeded and finely chopped

10 fl oz/300 ml/1 1/2 cups
   olive oil

method

Place the egg in a food processor or blender, add the mustard and salt and process for 30 seconds.

Add the lemon juice, cilantro, and chili and process briefly.

With the motor still running, add the olive oil through the feeder tube in a thin, steady stream. The mixture will thicken after half the oil has been added.

Continue adding the remaining oil until it is all absorbed. Transfer to a serving bowl, cover, and let chill in the refrigerator for 30 minutes to allow the flavors to develop before serving.

mole verde

ingredients

SERVES 4–6

9 oz/250 g/2¼ cups toasted
    pumpkin seeds
1¾ pints/1 litre/4 cups
    chicken stock
several pinches of ground
    cloves
8–10 tomatillos, diced, or use
    8 fl oz/225 ml/1⅓ cups
    mild tomatillo salsa
½ onion, chopped
½ fresh green chili, seeded
    and diced
3 garlic cloves, chopped
½ tsp. fresh thyme leaves
½ tsp. fresh marjoram leaves
3 tbsp. shortening or
    vegetable oil
3 bay leaves
4 tbsp. chopped fresh cilantro
salt and pepper
fresh green chili slices,
    to garnish

method

Grind the toasted pumpkin seeds in a food processor.
Add half the stock, the cloves, tomatillos, onion, chili,
garlic, thyme, and marjoram and blend to a purée.

Heat the shortening in a heavy-bottomed skillet and add
the puréed pumpkin seed mixture and the bay leaves.
Cook over medium–high heat for 5 minutes, or until the
mixture begins to thicken.

Remove the skillet from the heat and add the remaining
stock and the cilantro. Return the skillet to the heat and
cook until the sauce thickens, then remove from the heat.

Remove the bay leaves and place the sauce in a food
processor or blender and process until completely
smooth. Add salt and pepper to taste.

Transfer to a serving bowl, garnish with chili slices,
and serve.

mole poblano

ingredients

SERVES 4

3 dried mulato chilies

3 mild dried ancho chilies

5–6 dried New Mexico or
 California chilies

1 onion, chopped

5 garlic cloves, chopped

1 lb/450 g ripe tomatoes

2 tortillas, preferably stale, cut
 into small pieces

pinch of cloves

pinch of fennel seeds

1/8 tsp. each ground cinnamon,
 coriander, and cumin

3 tbsp. lightly toasted sesame
 seeds or tahini

3 tbsp. slivered or coarsely
 ground blanched almonds

2 tbsp. raisins

1 tbsp. peanut butter (optional)

16 fl oz/450 ml/2 cups
 chicken stock

3–4 tbsp. grated semisweet
 chocolate, plus extra
 to garnish

2 tbsp. mild chili powder

3 tbsp. vegetable oil

salt and pepper

about 1 tbsp. lime juice

method

Using metal tongs, roast each chili over an open flame for a few seconds until the color darkens on all sides. Alternatively, roast in an unoiled skillet over medium heat for 30 seconds, turning constantly.

Place the roasted chilies in a heatproof bowl or a pan and pour over enough boiling water to cover. Cover with a lid and let soften for at least 1 hour or overnight. Once or twice, lift the lid and rearrange the chilies so that they soak evenly.

Remove the softened chilies with a slotted spoon. Discard the stalks and seeds and cut the flesh into pieces. Place in a food processor or blender.

Add the onion, garlic, tomatoes, tortillas, cloves, fennel seeds, cinnamon, coriander, cumin, sesame seeds, almonds, raisins, and peanut butter, if using, then process to combine. With the motor running, add enough stock through the feed tube to make a smooth paste. Stir in the remaining stock, chocolate, and chili powder.

Heat the oil in a heavy-bottomed pan until it is smoking, then pour in the mole mixture. It will splatter and pop as it hits the hot oil. Cook for 10 minutes, stirring occasionally to prevent it burning.

Season to taste with salt, pepper, and lime juice, garnish with a little grated chocolate, and serve.

mild red chili sauce

ingredients

MAKES ABOUT 1¹/₂ CUPS

5 large fresh mild chilies, such
as New Mexico or ancho
16 fl oz/450 ml/2 cups
vegetable or chicken stock
1 tbsp. masa harina or
1 crumbled corn tortilla,
puréed with enough water
to make a thin paste
large pinch of ground cumin
1–2 garlic cloves, finely
chopped
juice of 1 lime
salt (optional)

method

Using metal tongs, roast each chili over an open flame
for a few seconds until the color darkens on all sides.
Alternatively, place the chilies under a preheated hot
broiler, turning them frequently. Place the chilies in a
heatproof bowl and pour boiling water over them. Cover
and let the chilies cool.

Meanwhile, place the stock in a pan and bring to a simmer.
When the chilies have cooled and are swelled up and
softened, remove from the water. Remove the seeds,
then cut the flesh into pieces. Process to a purée in a
food processor or blender, then mix in the hot stock.

Place the chili and stock mixture in a pan. Add the masa
harina or puréed tortilla, cumin, garlic, and lime juice. Bring
to a boil and cook for a few minutes, stirring, until the sauce
has thickened. Add salt to taste, if necessary, and serve.

quick tomato sauce

ingredients

SERVES 4–6

2 tbsp. vegetable or olive oil

1 onion, thinly sliced

5 garlic cloves, thinly sliced

14 oz/400 g canned
    tomatoes, diced, plus their
    juices, or 1 lb 5 oz/600 g
    fresh diced tomatoes

several shakes of mild chili
    powder

1 1/2 cups vegetable stock

salt and pepper

method

Heat the oil in a large skillet. Add the onion and garlic and cook for 3 minutes, or until just softened, stirring constantly.

Add the tomatoes, chili powder to taste, and the stock. Cook over medium–high heat for 10 minutes, or until the tomatoes have reduced slightly and the flavor of the sauce is more concentrated.

Season the sauce to taste with salt and pepper. Serve the dish warm.

chipotle salsa

ingredients

MAKES ABOUT 2 CUPS

1 lb/450 g ripe juicy
   tomatoes, diced
3–5 garlic cloves, finely
   chopped
1/2 bunch fresh cilantro
   leaves, coarsely chopped
1 small onion, chopped
1–2 tsp. adobo marinade
   from canned chipotle
   chilies
1/2–1 tsp. sugar
lime juice, to taste
salt
pinch of ground cinnamon
   (optional)
pinch of ground allspice
   (optional)
pinch of ground cumin
   (optional)

method

Place the tomatoes, garlic, and cilantro in a food
processor or blender.

Process the mixture until smooth, then add the onion,
adobo marinade, and sugar.

Squeeze in lime juice to taste. Season to taste with salt,
then add the cinnamon, allspice, and cumin, if using.

Serve at once, or cover and chill until ready to serve,
although the salsa is at its best when served freshly made.

corn and red bell pepper salsa

ingredients

SERVES 4–6

1 lb/450 g canned corn
kernels

1 large red bell pepper, diced

1 garlic clove, crushed

1–2 tbsp. finely chopped
bottled jalapeño chilies,
or to taste

4 scallions, finely chopped

2 tbsp. lemon juice

1 tbsp. olive oil

1 tbsp. chopped fresh cilantro

salt

method

Drain the corn and place in a large, nonmetallic bowl.

Add the red bell pepper, garlic, chilies, scallions, lemon juice, oil, and chopped cilantro, then season to taste with salt and stir well to combine.

Cover and let chill in the refrigerator for at least 30 minutes to allow the flavors to develop before serving.

two classic salsas

ingredients

SERVES 4–6

jalapeño salsa

1 onion, finely chopped

2–3 garlic cloves, finely
chopped

4–6 tbsp. coarsely chopped
pickled jalapeño chilies

juice of 1/2 lemon

about 1/4 tsp. ground cumin

salt

salsa cruda

6–8 ripe tomatoes, finely
chopped

31/2 fl oz/100 ml/scant 1/2 cup
tomato juice

3–4 garlic cloves, finely
chopped

1/2–1 bunch fresh cilantro
leaves, coarsely chopped

pinch of sugar

3–4 fresh green chilies, such
as jalapeño or serrano,
seeded and finely chopped

1/2–1 tsp. ground cumin

3–4 scallions, finely chopped

salt

method

To make the jalapeño salsa, place the onion in a
nonmetallic bowl with the garlic, chilies, lemon juice,
and cumin. Season to taste with salt and stir together.
Cover and chill until required.

To make a chunky-textured salsa cruda, stir all the
ingredients together in a nonmetallic bowl, adding salt to
taste. Cover and chill until required.

To make a smoother-textured salsa, process the
ingredients in a food processor or blender. Cover and
chill until required.

pico de gallo salsa

ingredients

SERVES 4–6

3 large, ripe tomatoes

1/2 red onion, finely chopped

1 large fresh green chili, such
as jalapeño, seeded and
finely chopped

2 tbsp. chopped fresh cilantro

juice of 1 lime, or to taste

salt and pepper

method

Halve the tomatoes, scoop out and discard the seeds, and dice the flesh. Place the flesh in a large, nonmetallic bowl.

Add the onion, chili, chopped cilantro and lime juice. Season to taste with salt and pepper and stir gently to combine.

Cover and let chill in the refrigerator for at least 30 minutes to allow the flavors to develop before serving.

pineapple & mango salsa

ingredients

SERVES 4

1/2 ripe pineapple
1 ripe mango
2 tbsp. chopped fresh mint
2 tsp. brown sugar
juice of 1 lime
1–2 tsp. Tabasco sauce or
    Habañero sauce, or
    to taste
1 large tomato, seeded
    and diced
salt

method

Slice the pineapple, then peel the slices and remove the cores. Dice the flesh and place in a nonmetallic bowl with any juice.

Slice the mango lengthwise on either side of the flat central seed. Peel the 2 mango pieces and dice the flesh. Slice and peel any remaining flesh around the seed, then dice. Add to the pineapple with any juice.

Add the chopped mint, sugar, lime juice, Tabasco, and tomato, then season to taste with salt and stir well to combine. Cover and let chill in the refrigerator for at least 30 minutes to allow the flavors to develop. Stir again before serving.

summer squash with green chilies & corn

ingredients

SERVES 4–6

2 corn cobs

2 small zucchini or other green summer squash, such as pattypans, cubed or sliced

2 small yellow summer squash, cubed or sliced

2 tbsp. butter

3 garlic cloves, finely chopped

3–4 large ripe flavorful tomatoes, diced

several pinches of mild chili powder

several pinches of ground cumin

1/2 fresh green chili, such as jalapeño, seeded and chopped

pinch of sugar

salt and pepper

method

Bring about 2 inches/5 cm of water to a boil in the bottom of a steamer. Add the corn, zucchini, and summer squash to the top part of the steamer, cover, and steam for about 3 minutes, depending on their maturity and freshness. Alternatively, blanch in a pan of boiling salted water for 3 minutes, then drain. Set aside until cool enough to handle. Using a large knife, slice the kernels off the cobs and set aside.

Melt the butter in a heavy-bottomed skillet. Add the garlic and cook for 1 minute to soften. Add the tomatoes, chili powder, cumin, chili, and sugar. Season to taste with salt and pepper and cook for a few minutes, or until the flavors have mingled.

Add the corn kernels, zucchini, and squash. Cook for 2 minutes, stirring, to warm through. Serve at once.

zucchini & summer squash with chorizo

ingredients

SERVES 4

2 zucchini, thinly sliced

2 yellow summer squash, thinly sliced

salt and pepper

2 fresh chorizo sausages, diced or sliced

3 garlic cloves, finely chopped

juice of $1/2$–1 lime

1–2 tbsp. chopped fresh cilantro

method

Cook the zucchini and summer squash in a pan of boiling salted water for 3–4 minutes, or until they are just tender. Drain well.

Brown the chorizo in a heavy-bottomed skillet, stirring with a spoon to break up into pieces. Pour off any excess fat from the browned chorizo, then add the garlic and blanched zucchini and summer squash. Cook for a few minutes, stirring gently, to combine the flavors.

Stir in the lime juice to taste. Season to taste with salt and pepper and serve at once sprinkled with chopped cilantro.

zucchini with green chili vinaigrette

ingredients

SERVES 4

1 large fresh mild green chili or a combination of 1 green bell pepper and 1/2–1 fresh green chili

4 zucchini, sliced

2–3 garlic cloves, finely chopped

pinch of sugar

1/4 tsp. ground cumin

2 tbsp. white wine vinegar

4 tbsp. extra-virgin olive oil

2–3 tbsp. chopped fresh cilantro

salt and pepper

4 ripe tomatoes, diced or sliced

tortilla chips, to serve (optional)

method

Roast the chili, or the combination of the green bell pepper and chili, in an unoiled heavy-bottomed skillet or under a preheated hot broiler until the skin is charred. Place in a plastic bag, twist to seal well, and let stand for 20 minutes.

Peel the skin from the chili and bell pepper, if using, then remove the seeds and slice the flesh. Set aside.

Bring about 2 inches/5 cm of water to a boil in the bottom of a steamer. Add the zucchini to the top part of the steamer, cover, and steam for 5 minutes, or until just tender.

Meanwhile, thoroughly combine the garlic, sugar, cumin, vinegar, oil, and cilantro in a bowl. Stir in the chili and bell pepper, if using, then season to taste with salt and pepper.

Arrange the zucchini and tomatoes in a serving bowl or on a platter and spoon over the chili dressing. Toss gently and serve with tortilla chips, if wished.

potatoes with chipotle cream

ingredients

SERVES 4

2 lb 12 oz/1.25 kg baking potatoes, peeled and cut into chunks

pinch of salt

pinch of sugar

7 fl oz/200 ml/3/4 cup sour cream

4 fl oz/120 ml/1/2 cup vegetable or chicken stock

3 garlic cloves, finely chopped

few shakes of bottled chipotle salsa or 1/2 dried chipotle, reconstituted, seeded, and thinly sliced

8 oz/225 g goat cheese, sliced

6 oz/175 g mozzarella or Cheddar cheese, grated

13/4 oz/50 g Parmesan or romano cheese, grated

method

Preheat the oven to 350°F/180°C. Place the potatoes in a pan of water with the salt and sugar. Bring to a boil and cook for 10 minutes, or until they are half cooked.

Combine the sour cream with the stock, garlic, and the chipotle salsa in a bowl.

Arrange half the potatoes in a flameproof casserole. Pour half the sour cream sauce over the potatoes and cover with the goat cheese slices. Top with the remaining potatoes and the sauce.

Sprinkle with the grated mozzarella or Cheddar cheese, then with either the grated Parmesan or romano cheese.

Bake in the oven for 30 minutes, or until the potatoes are tender and the cheese topping is lightly golden and crisp in places. Serve at once.

potatoes in green sauce

ingredients

SERVES 6

2 lb 4 oz/1 kg small waxy
    potatoes, peeled
salt
1 onion, halved and unpeeled
8 garlic cloves, unpeeled
1 fresh green chili
8 tomatillos, outer husks
    removed, or small tart
    tomatoes
8 fl oz/225 ml/1 cup chicken,
    meat, or vegetable stock,
    preferably homemade
1/2 tsp. ground cumin
1 fresh thyme sprig or
    generous pinch of dried
    thyme
1 fresh oregano sprig or
    generous pinch of dried
    oregano
2 tbsp. vegetable or virgin
    olive oil
1 zucchini, coarsely chopped
1 bunch fresh cilantro,
    chopped

method

Place the potatoes in a pan of salted water. Bring to a boil and cook for 15 minutes, or until almost tender. Do not overcook them. Drain and set aside.

Lightly char the onion, garlic, chili, and tomatillos or tomatoes in an unoiled heavy-bottomed skillet. Set aside. When cool enough to handle, peel and chop the onion, garlic, and chili; chop the tomatillos or tomatoes. Place in a food processor or blender with half the stock and process to form a purée. Add the cumin, thyme, and oregano and stir well to combine.

Heat the oil in the heavy-bottomed skillet. Add the purée and cook for 5 minutes, stirring, to reduce slightly and concentrate the flavors.

Add the potatoes and zucchini to the purée and pour in the rest of the stock. Add about half the cilantro and cook for an additional 5 minutes, or until the zucchini are tender.

Transfer to a serving bowl and serve sprinkled with the remaining chopped cilantro to garnish.

citrus salad with pomegranate

ingredients

SERVES 4

1 large pomegranate

1 grapefruit

2 sweet oranges

finely grated rind of 1/2 lime

1–2 garlic cloves, finely
   chopped

3 tbsp. red wine vinegar

juice of 2 limes

1/2 tsp. sugar

1/4 tsp. dry mustard

salt and pepper

4–5 tbsp. extra-virgin olive oil

1 head red leafy lettuce, such
   as oak leaf, washed and
   dried

1 avocado, pitted, peeled,
   diced, and tossed with a
   little lime juice

1/2 red onion, thinly sliced,
   to garnish

method

Cut the pomegranate into fourths, then press back the outer skin to push out the seeds into a bowl.

Using a sharp knife, cut a slice off the top and bottom of the grapefruit, then remove the peel and pith, cutting downward. Cut out the segments from between the membranes, then add to the pomegranate.

Finely grate the rind of half an orange and set aside. Using a sharp knife, cut a slice off the top and bottom of both oranges, then remove the peel and pith, cutting downward and taking care to retain the shape of the oranges. Slice horizontally into slices, then cut into fourths. Add the oranges to the pomegranate and grapefruit and stir to mix well.

Combine the reserved orange rind with the lime rind, garlic, vinegar, lime juice, sugar, and mustard in a small nonmetallic bowl. Season to taste with salt and pepper, then whisk in the oil.

Place the lettuce leaves in a serving bowl, then top with the fruit mixture and the avocado. Pour over the dressing and toss gently. Garnish with the onion rings and serve at once.

papaya, avocado & red bell pepper salad

ingredients

SERVES 4–6

7 oz/200 g mixed salad greens
2–3 scallions, chopped
3–4 tbsp. chopped fresh
  cilantro
1 small papaya
2 red bell peppers
1 avocado
1 tbsp. lime juice
3–4 tbsp. pumpkin seeds,
  preferably toasted
  (optional)

dressing

juice of 1 lime
large pinch of paprika
large pinch of ground cumin
large pinch of sugar
1 garlic clove, finely chopped
4 tbsp. extra-virgin olive oil
salt
dash of white wine vinegar
  (optional)

method

Combine the salad greens with the scallions and cilantro in a bowl. Mix well, then transfer the salad to a large serving dish.

Cut the papaya in half and scoop out the seeds with a spoon. Cut into fourths, remove the peel, and slice the flesh. Arrange on top of the salad greens. Cut the bell peppers in half, remove the cores and seeds, then thinly slice. Add the bell peppers to the salad greens.

Cut the avocado in half around the pit. Twist apart, then remove the pit with a knife. Carefully peel off the skin, dice the flesh, and toss in lime juice to prevent discoloration. Add to the other salad ingredients.

To make the dressing, whisk the lime juice, paprika, cumin, sugar, garlic, and oil together in a small bowl. Season to taste with salt.

Pour the dressing over the salad and toss lightly, adding a dash of wine vinegar if a flavor with more "bite" is preferred. Sprinkle with pumpkin seeds, if using.

mexican
potato salad

ingredients

SERVES 4

2 lb 12 oz/1.25 kg waxy
   potatoes, sliced
1 ripe avocado
1 tsp. olive oil
1 tsp. lemon juice
1 garlic clove, crushed
1 onion, chopped
2 large tomatoes, sliced
1 fresh green chili, seeded
   and chopped
1 yellow bell pepper, seeded
   and sliced
2 tbsp. chopped fresh cilantro
salt and pepper
lemon wedges, to garnish

method

Cook the potato slices in a pan of boiling water for 10–15 minutes, or until tender. Drain and let cool.

Meanwhile, cut the avocado in half, remove the pit and peel. Mash the avocado flesh with a fork (you could also scoop the avocado flesh from the 2 halves using a spoon and then mash it).

Add the olive oil, lemon juice, garlic, and chopped onion to the avocado flesh and stir to mix. Cover the bowl with plastic wrap, to minimize discoloration, and set aside.

Combine the tomatoes, green chili, and yellow bell pepper and transfer to a salad bowl with the potato slices.

Arrange the avocado mixture on top of the salad and sprinkle with the chopped fresh cilantro. Season to taste with salt and pepper and serve the salad immediately, garnished with lemon wedges.

green bean salad with feta cheese

ingredients

SERVES 4

12 oz/350 g green beans

1 red onion, chopped

3–4 tbsp. chopped fresh
  cilantro

2 radishes, thinly sliced

2³/₄ oz/75 g feta cheese
  (drained weight), crumbled

1 tsp. chopped fresh oregano,
  plus extra leaves to garnish
  (optional), or ¹/₂ tsp. dried

pepper

2 tbsp. red wine or fruit vinegar

3 fl oz/80 ml/¹/₃ cup extra-
  virgin olive oil

3 ripe tomatoes, cut into
  wedges

method

Bring about 2 inches/5 cm of water to a boil in the bottom
of a steamer. Add the beans to the top part of the steamer,
cover, and steam for 5 minutes, or until just tender.

Place the beans in a large bowl and add the onion, cilantro,
radishes, and feta cheese.

Sprinkle the oregano over the salad, then season to taste
with pepper. Mix the vinegar and oil together in a small
bowl and pour over the salad. Toss gently to mix well.

Transfer to a serving platter, surround with the tomato
wedges, and serve at once, or cover and chill until ready
to serve.

rice with lime

ingredients

SERVES 4

2 tbsp. vegetable oil

1 small onion, finely chopped

3 garlic cloves, finely chopped

6 oz/175 g/ scant 1 cup long-
grain rice

16 fl oz/450 ml/2 cups
chicken or vegetable stock

juice of 1 lime

1 tbsp. chopped fresh cilantro

sautéed plantain, to garnish
(optional)

lime wedges, to serve
(optional)

method

Heat the oil in a flameproof casserole or heavy-bottomed pan. Add the onion and garlic and cook gently, stirring occasionally, for 2 minutes. Add the rice and cook for an additional minute, stirring. Pour in the stock, increase the heat, and bring the rice to a boil. Reduce the heat to a very low simmer.

Cover and cook the rice for 10 minutes, or until the rice is just tender and the liquid is absorbed.

Sprinkle in the lime juice and fork the rice to fluff up and to mix in the juice. Sprinkle with the cilantro, then garnish with sautéed plantain and serve with lime wedges, if wished.

spicy rice

ingredients

SERVES 4

3 tbsp. olive oil

6 scallions, chopped

1 celery stalk, finely chopped

3 garlic cloves, finely chopped

2 green bell peppers, seeded
and chopped

corn kernels, cut from 1 ear
fresh corn

2 fresh mild green chilies,
seeded and finely chopped

9 oz/250 g/generous 1¼
cups long-grain rice

2 tsp. ground cumin

1 pint/600 ml/2½ cups
chicken or vegetable stock

2 tbsp. chopped fresh cilantro

salt and pepper

fresh cilantro sprigs,
to garnish

method

Heat the oil in a large, heavy-bottom pan over medium heat. Add the scallions, celery, and garlic and cook for 5 minutes, or until softened. Add the bell peppers, corn, and chilies and cook for 5 minutes.

Add the rice and cumin and cook, stirring to coat the grains in the oil, for 2 minutes.

Stir in the stock and half the chopped cilantro and bring to a boil. Reduce the heat, cover, and let simmer for 15 minutes, or until nearly all the liquid has been absorbed and the rice is just tender.

Remove from the heat and fluff up with a fork. Stir in the remaining chopped cilantro and season to taste with salt and pepper. Let stand, covered, for 5 minutes before serving. Serve garnished with cilantro sprigs.

rice with black beans

ingredients

SERVES 4

1 onion, chopped

5 garlic cloves, chopped

8 fl oz/225 ml/1 cup chicken or vegetable stock

2 tbsp. vegetable oil

6 oz/175 g/scant 1 cup long-grain rice

8 fl oz/225 ml/1 cup liquid from cooking black beans, plus a few beans

$1/2$ tsp. ground cumin

salt and pepper

to garnish

3–5 scallions, thinly sliced

2 tbsp. chopped fresh cilantro

method

Place the onion in a food processor or blender with the garlic and stock and process until the consistency of a chunky sauce.

Heat the oil in a heavy-bottomed skillet and cook the rice until it is golden. Add the onion mixture with the cooking liquid from the black beans and any beans. Add the cumin and salt and pepper to taste.

Cover the skillet and cook over medium–low heat for 10 minutes, or until the rice is just tender. The rice should be a pinkish-gray color and taste delicious.

Fluff up the rice with a fork, then cover and let stand for 5 minutes. Serve sprinkled with thinly sliced scallions and chopped cilantro.

green rice

ingredients

SERVES 4

1–2 onions, halved and
    unpeeled
6–8 large garlic cloves,
    unpeeled
1 large mild fresh chili or
    1 green bell pepper and
    1 small fresh green chili
1 bunch fresh cilantro leaves,
    chopped
8 fl oz/225 ml/1 cup chicken
    or vegetable stock
3 fl oz/80 ml/$\frac{1}{3}$ cup vegetable
    or olive oil
6 oz/175 g/scant 1 cup long-
    grain rice
salt and pepper
fresh cilantro sprig, to garnish

method

Heat an unoiled heavy-bottomed skillet and cook the onion, garlic, chili, and bell pepper, if using, until lightly charred on all sides, including the cut sides of the onions. Cover and let cool.

When cool enough to handle, remove the skin and seeds from the chili and bell pepper, if using. Chop the flesh.

Remove the skins from the cooled onion and garlic and finely chop.

Place the vegetables in a food processor or blender with the chopped cilantro leaves and stock, then process to a smooth thin purée.

Heat the oil in a heavy-bottomed pan. Add the rice and cook until it is glistening and lightly browned in places, stirring to prevent it burning. Add the vegetable purée, cover, and cook over medium–low heat for 10–15 minutes, or until the rice is just tender.

Fluff up the rice with a fork, then cover and let stand for 5 minutes. Adjust the seasoning, garnish with a cilantro sprig, and serve.

mexican beans

ingredients

SERVES 4

1 lb 2 oz/500 g/3 cups dried
    pinto or pink beans
1 fresh mint sprig
1 fresh thyme sprig
1 fresh flatleaf parsley sprig
1 onion, cut into chunks
salt
shredded scallion, to garnish
warmed flour tortillas (see
    page 206) or soft corn
    tortillas, to serve

method

Pick through the beans and remove any bits of grit or stone. Cover the beans with cold water and let soak overnight. If you want to cut down on soaking time, bring the beans to a boil in a pan, cook for 5 minutes, then remove from the heat and let stand, covered, for 2 hours.

Drain the beans, place in a pan, and cover with fresh water. Add the herb sprigs. Bring to a boil, then reduce the heat to very low and cook gently, covered, for 2 hours, or until the beans are tender. The best way to check that they are done is to sample a bean or two every so often after $1^3/_4$ hours' cooking time.

Add the onion chunks and continue to cook until the onion and beans are very tender.

To serve as a side dish, drain, season to taste with salt, and serve in a bowl lined with warmed tortillas, garnished with shredded scallion.

refried beans

ingredients

SERVES 4

8 oz/225 g/1¹/₃ cups dried
   pinto beans, soaked
   overnight and drained
2 onions, 1 quartered and
   1 chopped
1 chopped and 1 whole
   bay leaf
1 fresh thyme sprig
1 dried red chili, such as
   ancho
3 tbsp. olive oil
2 tsp. ground cumin
3 oz/85 g Cheddar cheese,
   grated (optional)

method

Place the beans in a large pan with the quartered onion, the herbs, and chili. Pour over enough cold water to cover and bring to a boil. Reduce the heat, cover, and let simmer gently for 2 hours, or until the beans are very tender.

Drain the beans, reserving the cooking liquid, and discard the onion, herbs, and chili.

Place two-thirds of the beans with the cooking liquid in a food processor or blender and process until coarsely blended.

Heat the oil in a heavy-bottom skillet over medium heat. Add the chopped onion and cook for 10 minutes, or until soft and golden. Add the cumin and cook, stirring, for 2 minutes. Stir in the puréed and reserved beans and cook, stirring constantly, until the liquid reduces and the mixture thickens. Stir in the grated cheese, if using, and cook, stirring, until melted. Serve at once.

chilied cornbread

ingredients

SERVES 8

5 oz/140 g/scant 1 cup
   cornmeal
2 1/2 oz/70 g/scant 1/2 cup all-
   purpose flour
3 tsp. baking powder
1 small onion, finely chopped
1–2 fresh green chilies, such
   as jalapeño, seeded and
   chopped
4 tbsp. corn or vegetable oil
4 1/2 oz/125 g canned
   creamed-style corn
   kernels
8 fl oz/225 ml/1 cup sour
   cream
2 eggs, beaten

method

Preheat the oven to 350°F/180°C.

Place the cornmeal, flour, and baking powder in a large bowl, then stir in the onion and chili.

Heat the oil in a 9-inch/23-cm heavy-bottom skillet with a heatproof handle, tipping the skillet to coat the bottom and sides with the oil.

Make a well in the center of the ingredients in the bowl. Add the corn, sour cream, and eggs, then pour in the hot oil from the skillet. Stir lightly until combined. Pour into the hot skillet and smooth the surface.

Bake in the preheated oven for 35–40 minutes, or until a wooden toothpick inserted into the center comes out clean. Cut into wedges and serve warm from the skillet.

flour tortillas

ingredients

MAKES 12

12 oz/350 g/2¼ cups all-purpose flour, plus extra for dusting

1 tsp. salt

½ tsp. baking powder

2¾ oz/75 g shortening or white vegetable fat, diced

about 4 fl oz/125 ml/½ cup hot water

method

Sift the flour, salt, and baking powder into a large bowl. Add the shortening and rub it in with your fingertips until the mixture resembles fine bread crumbs. Add enough water to form a soft dough.

Turn out the dough on to a lightly floured counter and knead until smooth. Divide the dough into 12 pieces and shape each into a ball. Cover with a clean dish towel and let rest for 15 minutes.

Roll out 1 ball at a time, keeping the remainder of the dough covered, into an 7-inch/18-cm circle. Stack the tortillas between sheets of nonstick parchment paper.

Heat a grill pan or large, heavy-bottom skillet over medium-high heat. Cook 1 tortilla at a time for 1–2 minutes on each side, or until lightly browned in places and puffed up. Serve warm.

to finish

After the hearty and satisfying fare that is characteristic of Mexico, you might find that all you want to finish your meal is some fresh fruit, served Mexican-style with a splash of tequila or a squeeze of lime to flavor it. If you need something to counter the effects of the hot spices, serve the fruit frozen and whipped into a "blizzard" or made into a refreshing sherbet. An incredible variety of fruits are grown in Mexico, from citrus fruits to melons and pineapples, mangoes and papaya, peaches and plums – just choose your favorite.

Those with a very sweet tooth will find plenty to satisfy their cravings – a delicious chocolate creme caramel, melt-in-the-mouth chocolate meringues, pastries bursting with fruity fillings, or puffy deep-fried bunuelos, a sort of doughnut, served in a puddle of orange-cinnamon syrup. There is also the light and wonderful *torta de cielo* – it is surely impossible to resist anything with a name that translates into "cake of heaven" and tastes as good as it sounds.

There are some interesting blends of ingredients here and there – Mexican bread pudding is topped with cheese, for example, and if you're a fan of chocolate-chip ice cream, beware, because that unique chocolate/chili combo creeps in here, too!

icy fruit blizzard

ingredients

SERVES 4

1 pineapple

1 large piece seeded
watermelon, peeled and
cut into small pieces

8 oz/225 g/1^1/$_2$ cups
strawberries or other
berries, hulled and left
whole or sliced

1 mango, peach, or nectarine,
peeled and sliced

1 banana, peeled and sliced

orange juice

superfine sugar, to taste

method

Cover 2 nonstick cookie sheets or ordinary cookie sheets with a sheet of plastic wrap. Arrange the fruits on top and open freeze for at least 2 hours, or until firm and icy.

Place one type of fruit in a food processor and process until it is all broken up into small pieces.

Add a little orange juice and sugar to taste, and continue to process until it forms a granular mixture. Repeat with the remaining fruits. Arrange in chilled bowls and serve immediately.

guava, lime, & tequila sherbet

ingredients

SERVES 4

6 oz/175 g/scant 1 cup
   superfine sugar

15 fl oz/425 ml/scant 2 cups
   water

4 fresh ripe guavas or 8 canned
   guava halves

2 tbsp. tequila

juice of 1/2 lime, or to taste

1 egg white

method

Heat the sugar and water in a heavy-bottom pan over low heat until the sugar has dissolved. When the liquid turns clear, boil for 5 minutes, or until a thick syrup forms. Remove the pan from the heat and let cool.

Cut the fresh guavas, if using, in half. Scoop out the flesh. Discard the seeds from the fresh or canned guava flesh. Transfer to a food processor or blender and process until smooth.

Add the purée to the syrup with the tequila and lime juice to taste. Transfer the mixture to a freezerproof container and freeze for 1 hour, or until slushy.

Remove from the freezer and process again until smooth. Return to the freezer and freeze until firm. Process again until smooth. With the motor still running, add the egg white through the feeder tube. Freeze until solid.

Transfer the sherbet to the refrigerator 15 minutes before serving. Serve in scoops.

chocolate chip
& chili ice cream

ingredients

SERVES 4

1 egg

1 egg yolk

2 oz/55 g/generous 1/4 cup
superfine sugar

51/2 oz/150 g semisweet
chocolate, finely chopped

18 fl oz/500 ml/scant 21/2
cups milk

1 dried red chili, such as ancho

1 vanilla bean

18 fl oz/500 ml/scant
21/2cups heavy cream

51/2 oz150 g//scant 1 cup
semisweet, milk, or white
chocolate chips

method

Place the egg, egg yolk, and sugar in a heatproof bowl set over a pan of simmering water. Beat until light and fluffy.

Place the chopped chocolate, milk, chili, and vanilla bean in a separate pan and heat gently until the chocolate has dissolved and the milk is almost boiling. Pour onto the egg mixture, discarding the chili and vanilla bean, and beat well. Let cool.

Lightly whip the cream in a separate bowl. Fold into the cold mixture with the chocolate chips. Transfer to an ice cream machine and process for 15 minutes, or according to the manufacturer's instructions. Alternatively, transfer to a freezerproof container and freeze for 1 hour, or until partially frozen. Remove from the freezer, transfer to a bowl, and beat to break down the ice crystals. Freeze again for 30 minutes, then beat again. Freeze once more until firm.

Transfer the ice cream to the refrigerator 15 minutes before serving. Serve in scoops.

mexican chocolate crème caramel

ingredients

SERVES 4

4 oz/115 g/generous 1/2 cup
   granulated sugar
4 tbsp. water
1 pint/600 ml/2 1/2 cups milk
2 oz/55 g semisweet
   chocolate, grated
4 eggs
2 tbsp. superfine sugar
1 tsp. vanilla extract

method

Preheat the oven to 325°F/160°C. Place a 4-cup soufflé dish in the oven to heat.

Place the granulated sugar and water in a heavy-bottom pan over low heat. Stir until the sugar has dissolved. Bring to a boil, without stirring, and boil until caramelized. Pour into the hot dish, tipping it to coat the bottom and sides. Let cool.

Place the milk and grated chocolate in a separate pan and heat, stirring occasionally, until the chocolate has dissolved.

Meanwhile, beat the eggs and superfine sugar together in a bowl with a wooden spoon. Gradually beat in the chocolate milk. Add the vanilla extract. Strain into the prepared dish.

Stand the dish in a roasting pan and fill the pan with enough lukewarm water to come halfway up the sides of the dish. Bake in the preheated oven for 1 hour, or until set. Let cool, then invert onto a serving plate. Let chill in the refrigerator before serving.

oranges & strawberries with lime

ingredients

SERVES 4

3 sweet oranges

8 oz/225 g/1½ cups strawberries

grated rind and juice of 1 lime

1–2 tbsp. superfine sugar

to decorate

fine lime rind strips

fresh mint sprig

method

Using a sharp knife, cut a slice off the top and bottom of the oranges, then remove the peel and pith, cutting downward and taking care to retain the shape of the oranges.

Using a small sharp knife, cut down between the membranes of the oranges to remove the segments. Discard the membranes.

Hull the strawberries, pulling the leaves off with a pinching action. Cut into slices, along the length of the strawberries.

Place the oranges and strawberries in a nonmetallic bowl, then sprinkle with the lime rind and juice and sugar. Cover and chill until ready to serve.

To serve, transfer to a serving bowl. Decorate the dish with lime rind strips and a mint sprig.

aztec oranges

ingredients

SERVES 4–6

6 oranges
1 lime
2 tbsp. tequila
2 tbsp. orange-flavored
    liqueur
brown sugar, to taste
fine lime rind strips,
    to decorate

method

Using a sharp knife, cut a slice off the top and bottom of the oranges, then remove the peel and pith, cutting downward and taking care to retain the shape of the oranges.

Holding the oranges on their side, cut them horizontally into slices.

Place the oranges in a nonmetallic bowl. Cut the lime in half and squeeze over the oranges. Sprinkle with the tequila and liqueur, then sprinkle over sugar to taste.

Cover and chill until ready to serve, then transfer to a serving dish and garnish with lime rind strips.

pineapple with tequila & mint

ingredients

SERVES 4–6

1 ripe pineapple

sugar, to taste

juice of 1 lemon

2–3 tbsp. tequila or a few
drops of vanilla extract

several sprigs of fresh mint,
leaves removed and cut
into thin strips

fresh mint sprig, to decorate

method

Using a sharp knife, cut off the top and bottom of the pineapple. Place upright on a board, then slice off the skin, cutting downward. Cut in half, remove the core if wished, then cut the flesh into chunks.

Place the pineapple in a bowl and sprinkle with the sugar, lemon juice, and tequila or vanilla extract.

Toss the pineapple to coat well, then cover and chill until ready to serve.

To serve, arrange on a serving plate and sprinkle with the mint strips. Decorate the dish with a mint sprig.

bunuelos with orange-cinnamon syrup

ingredients

SERVES 4

8 oz/225 g/1 1/2 cups all-purpose flour, plus extra for dusting

1 tsp. baking powder

1/4 tsp. salt

1 tbsp. brown sugar

1 egg, beaten

2 tbsp. butter, melted

4 fl oz/125 ml/about 1/2 cup evaporated milk

vegetable oil, for deep-frying

for the orange-cinnamon syrup

12 fl oz/350 ml/1 1/2 cups water

grated rind of 1 small orange

4 tbsp. freshly squeezed orange juice

3 1/2 oz/100 g/1/2 cup brown sugar

1 tbsp. honey

2 tsp. ground cinnamon

method

Sift the flour, baking powder, and salt together into a large bowl. Stir in the sugar. Beat in the egg and butter with enough evaporated milk to form a soft, smooth dough.

Shape the dough into 8 balls. Cover and let rest for 30 minutes.

Meanwhile, to make the syrup, place the water, orange rind and juice, sugar, honey, and cinnamon in a heavy-bottom pan over medium heat. Bring to a boil, stirring constantly, then reduce the heat and let simmer gently for 20 minutes, or until thickened.

Flatten the dough balls to make cakes. Heat the oil for deep-frying in a deep-fryer or deep pan to 350–375°F/180–190°C, or until a cube of bread browns in 30 seconds. Deep-fry the bunuelos in batches for 4–5 minutes, turning once, or until golden brown and puffed. Remove with a slotted spoon and drain on paper towels. Serve with the syrup spooned over.

empanadas of banana & chocolate

ingredients

SERVES 4 – 6

about 8 sheets of phyllo
  pastry, cut in half
  lengthwise
melted butter or vegetable oil,
  for brushing
2 ripe sweet bananas
1–2 tsp. sugar
juice of 1/4 lemon
6–7 oz/175–200 g semisweet
  chocolate, broken into
  small pieces
confectioners' sugar, for dusting
ground cinnamon, for dusting

method

Preheat the oven to 375°F/190°C. Working one at a time, lay a long rectangular sheet of phyllo out in front of you and brush it with butter.

Peel and dice the bananas and place in a bowl. Add the sugar and lemon juice and stir well to combine. Stir in the chocolate.

Place a couple of teaspoons of the banana and chocolate mixture in one corner of the dough, then fold over into a triangle shape to enclose the filling. Continue to fold in a triangular shape, until the phyllo is completely wrapped around the filling.

Dust the pockets with confectioners' sugar and cinnamon. Place on a cookie sheet and continue the process with the remaining phyllo and filling.

Bake in the oven for 15 minutes, or until the pastries are golden. Remove from the oven and serve hot—warn people that the filling is very hot.

peach & pecan empanadas

ingredients

MAKES 8

12 oz/350 g ready-made puff
    pastry, thawed if frozen
all-purpose flour, for dusting
3 fresh peaches
5 fl oz/150 ml/²/₃ cup sour
    cream
4 tbsp. brown sugar
4 tbsp. pecan halves, toasted
    and finely chopped
beaten egg, to glaze
superfine sugar, for sprinkling

method

Preheat the oven to 400°F/200°C. Roll out the pastry on a lightly floured counter. Using a 6-inch/15-cm saucer as a guide, cut out 8 circles.

Place the peaches in a heatproof bowl and pour over enough boiling water to cover. Let stand for a few seconds, then drain and peel off the skins. Halve the peaches, remove the pits, and slice the flesh.

Place a spoonful of sour cream on one half of each pastry circle and top with a few peach slices. Sprinkle over a little brown sugar and some nuts. Brush each edge with a little beaten egg, fold the pastry over the filling, and press the edges together to seal. Crimp the edges with a fork and prick the tops.

Place on a baking sheet, brush with beaten egg, and sprinkle with superfine sugar. Bake in the preheated oven for 20 minutes, or until they turn golden brown.

churros

ingredients

SERVES 4

8 fl oz/225 ml/1 cup water

3 oz/85 g butter or
shortening, diced

2 tbsp. brown sugar

finely grated rind of 1 small
orange (optional)

pinch of salt

6 oz/175 g/1⅛ cups all-
purpose flour, well sifted

1 tsp. ground cinnamon, plus
extra for dusting

1 tsp. vanilla extract

2 eggs

vegetable oil, for deep-frying

superfine sugar, for dusting

method

Heat the water, butter, brown sugar, orange rind, if using, and salt in a heavy-bottom pan over medium heat until the butter has melted.

Add the flour, all at once, the cinnamon, and vanilla extract, then remove the pan from the heat and beat rapidly until the mixture pulls away from the side of the pan.

Let cool slightly, then beat in the eggs, one at a time, beating well after each addition, until the mixture is thick and smooth. Spoon into a pastry bag fitted with a wide star tip.

Heat the oil for deep-frying in a deep-fryer or deep pan to 350°–375°F/180°–190°C, or until a cube of bread browns in 30 seconds. Pipe 5-inch/13-cm lengths about 3 inches/7.5 cm apart into the oil. Deep-fry for 2 minutes on each side, or until golden brown. Remove with a slotted spoon and drain on paper towels. five Dust the churros with superfine sugar and cinnamon and serve.

mexican bread pudding

ingredients

SERVES 4

2 oz/55 g butter, plus extra for greasing

12 fl oz/350 ml/1^1/$_2$ cups water

8 oz/225 g/generous 1 cup brown sugar

1 cinnamon stick, broken

1 tsp. ground anise

2 oz/55 g/^{1}/$_3$ cup raisins

10 small slices bread

3 oz/85 g/^{3}/$_4$ cup shelled pecans, toasted and chopped

2 oz/55 g/^{1}/$_2$ cup slivered almonds, toasted

6 oz/175 g mild Cheddar cheese, grated

method

Preheat the oven to 375°F/190°C. Generously grease an ovenproof dish.

Heat the water, sugar, cinnamon stick, and anise in a pan over medium heat and stir constantly until the sugar has dissolved. Add the raisins and let simmer for 5 minutes without stirring.

Spread butter onto one side of each bread slice and arrange buttered-side up on a baking sheet. Bake in the preheated oven for 5 minutes, or until golden brown. Turn over and bake the other side for 5 minutes.

Line the base of the ovenproof dish with half the toast. Sprinkle over half the nuts and grated cheese. Remove and discard the cinnamon stick from the raisin mixture, then spoon half of the raisin mixture over the toast. Top with the remaining toast, nuts, grated cheese, and raisin mixture.

Bake in the preheated oven for 20–25 minutes, or until set and golden brown on top.

mexican chocolate meringues

ingredients

MAKES ABOUT 25 MERINGUES

4–5 egg whites, at room
    temperature
pinch of salt
$1/4$ tsp. cream of tartar
$1/4$–$1/2$ tsp. vanilla extract
6–7 oz/175–200 g/$3/4$–1 cup
    superfine sugar
$1/8$–$1/4$ tsp. ground cinnamon
4 oz/115 g semisweet
    chocolate, grated

to serve

ground cinnamon
generous 4 oz/115 g/$3/4$ cup
    strawberries
chocolate-flavored cream

method

Preheat the oven to 300°F/150°C. Whisk the egg whites until they are foamy, then add the salt and cream of tartar and beat until very stiff. Whisk in the vanilla extract, then slowly whisk in the sugar, a small amount at a time, until the meringue is shiny and stiff. This should take about 3 minutes by hand, and under a minute with an electric beater.

Whisk in the cinnamon and grated chocolate. Spoon mounds of about 2 tablespoonfuls on to an ungreased nonstick cookie sheet. Space the mounds well.

Bake in the preheated oven for 2 hours, or until set.

Carefully remove from the cookie sheet. If the meringues are too moist and soft, return them to the oven to firm up and dry out more. Let cool completely.

Serve the chocolate meringues dusted with ground cinnamon and accompanied by strawberries and chocolate-flavored cream.

mexican wedding cakes

ingredients

MAKES ABOUT 36

8 oz/225 g butter, softened

8 oz/225 g/2 cups
confectioners' sugar

1 tsp. vanilla extract

8 oz/225 g/1^1/$_2$ cups all-
purpose flour, plus extra
for dusting

^{1}/$_2$ tsp. salt

3^1/$_2$ oz/100 g/^{7}/$_8$ cup pecan or
walnut halves, toasted and
finely chopped

method

Cream the butter with half the sugar and vanilla extract in a large bowl. Sift the flour and salt together into the bowl and fold into the mixture. Stir in the nuts. Cover and let chill in the refrigerator for 1 hour, or until firm.

Preheat the oven to 375°F/190°C. With floured hands, shape the dough into 1-inch/2.5-cm balls and place about 1^1/$_2$ inches/4 cm apart on 2 large baking sheets.

Bake in the preheated oven for 10 minutes, or until set but not browned, rotating the baking sheets so that the cookies bake evenly. Let cool on the baking sheets for 2–3 minutes.

Place the remaining sugar in a shallow dish. Roll the warm cookies in the sugar, then let cool on wire racks for 30 minutes. When cold, roll again in the sugar. Store in airtight containers.

torta de cielo

ingredients

SERVES 4–6

8 oz/225 g/1 cup unsalted
butter, at room
temperature, plus extra for
greasing
6 oz/175 g/1¼ cups whole
almonds, in their skins
8 oz/225 g/1¼ cups sugar
3 eggs, lightly beaten
1 tsp. almond extract
1 tsp. vanilla extract
9 tbsp. all-purpose flour
pinch of salt

to decorate

confectioners' sugar,
for dusting
slivered almonds, toasted

method

Preheat the oven to 350°F/180°C. Lightly grease an
8-inch/20-cm round or square cake pan and line the
pan with parchment paper.

Place the almonds in a food processor and process to
form a "mealy" mixture. Set aside.

Beat the butter and sugar together in a large bowl until
smooth and fluffy. Beat in the eggs, almonds, and both
the almond and vanilla extracts until well blended.

Stir in the flour and salt and mix briefly, until the flour is
just incorporated.

Pour or spoon the batter into the prepared pan and
smooth the surface. Bake in the preheated oven for
40–50 minutes, or until the cake feels spongy when
gently pressed.

Remove from the oven and let stand on a wire rack
to cool. To serve, dust with confectioners' sugar and
decorate with toasted slivered almonds.